Retire on Less Than You Think

Retire on **Less** Than You Think

The New York Times

GUIDE TO PLANNING
YOUR FINANCIAL FUTURE

SECOND EDITION

FRED BROCK

TIMES BOOKS

HENRY HOLT AND COMPANY | NEW YORK

Times Books
Henry Holt and Company, LLC
Publishers since 1866
175 Fifth Avenue
New York, New York 10010
www.henryholt.com

Henry Holt® is a registered trademark of
Henry Holt and Company, LLC.

Library of Congress Cataloging-in-Publication Data

Brock, Fred.
    Retire on less than you think : the New York times guide to planning
your financial future / Fred Brock.— 2nd ed.
        p.   cm.
    Includes bibliographical references and index.
    ISBN-13: 978-0-8050-8730-7
    ISBN-10: 0-8050-8730-3
    1. Finance, Personal—United States.   2. Retirement—United States—Planning.
I. New York times.   II. Title.
    HG179.B7438   2008
    332.024'010—dc22   2007040161

First Edition 2004
Second Edition 2008

Designed by Kelly S. Too
Illustrations designed by Pat Lyons

Printed in the United States of America

P1

contents

preface

Since the first edition of this book was published in 2004, my life has changed considerably. It's as though I unconsciously wrote about my own future. Later that year, I took early retirement from the *New York Times,* and my wife and I moved to Kansas where I took a teaching post at Kansas State University. Although I did not retire, many of the dynamics of the move—which are explained in chapter 5—were the same. I ended up proving by my own example that *you can retire on less than you think*, especially if you are willing to relocate to a less expensive area of the country. We even generated enough money to buy a second, small home in southern Arizona, where we vacation and plan to eventually "retire," whatever that may come to mean.

Like its predecessor, this book is an outgrowth of the "Seniority" column I wrote for nearly six years for the *New York Times* Sunday "Money & Business" section. Writing the column and the two editions of the book has been an engaging process of learning and discovery, the results of which I hope will help people focus more clearly on some of the big issues they will face as they plan their retirements. For most of us, the main question is "Can I afford to retire?" On this central question there is an incredible disconnect between the everyday reality of how much it takes to live in retirement and how much money Wall Street and the mutual fund industry tell us we need. Unfortunately, much of the media have blithely accepted the inflated projections of financial services industry "experts." This misinformation has created a lot of needless worry for many people, sometimes causing them to delay retiring. I hope this book will serve as a balance to these self-serving projections and help people realize that retirement, however they define it, is not just a dream.

This book is intended neither as an investment guide nor as a self-improvement guide—except in the sense that your personal situation might be improved by retiring.

When calculating future earnings on savings, I have usually used a rate of 6.5 percent. I selected it because it seemed a middle ground between those optimists who see future stock returns of 12 to 15 percent and the doomsayers who see 2 percent or less. Also, many very sober economists foresee market returns of 5 to 7 percent over the next decade or so. With online calculators, readers can easily substitute their own rate.

Because of the lag time in book publishing, some figures cited may be slightly out of date. But in most cases it's the relative differences between sets of figures that are important; they will likely remain constant.

All the people described in these pages are real—with one exception. James McCain is not the actual name of the retired professor in chapter 2. He requested that I not use his name or other details that would identify him, in order to protect his privacy. I agreed because, ultimately, his story is more compelling than who he is. Everything else about him, including his personal financial information, is accurate.

I am grateful to the many people who helped me with this book and who were willing to discuss their personal finances. I would especially like to thank Bill and Donna Taaffe.

I would also like to thank my talented editor, Robin Dennis; my always supportive agent, Alice Martell; the *New York Times's* Pat

Lyons, who has created the graphics for all my books; and my colleagues at the A.Q. Miller School of Journalism and Mass Communications at Kansas State University and Angela Powers, its director, who have always been kind and helpful.

I will always be grateful to my wife, Evelyn, whose advice—editorial and otherwise—is usually on target.

Finally, thanks to Elton Pasea, the "happiest guy in Texas," whom you will meet in chapter 2. He continues to show the way.

Retire on Less Than You Think

1

Do You Really Want to Retire?

*In the twentieth century, we gained an additional thirty years of life.
It took the preceding fifty centuries to do that. That's extraordinary.*
—ROBERT N. BUTLER, M.D., PRESIDENT,
INTERNATIONAL LONGEVITY CENTER–USA

The basic idea behind this book is simple and straightforward: you can retire sooner and on less money than you think, and live quite well, if you are willing to make a few relatively painless lifestyle changes.

Various polls in recent years by AARP, the Employee Benefit Research Institute, and *USA Today* have shown that some 60 percent of working Americans dream of early retirement. Yet every time there is some jarring economic news—declining stock prices or a slump in the housing market—many people feel they must postpone retirement as they contemplate their shrinking investments and how much money they still need to save.

This is a book for those dreamers who want to retire sooner rather than later but are afraid they can't afford it: people who yearn for the time to realize a lifelong dream or avocation; people who have reached a dead end in their careers or who are burned out after years of doing the same thing and want to move on; or people who simply want a change. It is also for those who are at or past the traditional retirement age of sixty-five but continue to work because they are convinced they don't have enough money to retire.

Also, of course, it is for those who suddenly find themselves involuntarily retiring early because of employer cutbacks. Such forced retirements usually involve so-called incentive packages that may include a lump-sum payment or extra years credited to your retirement account—or both. Many forced retirees are equally apprehensive, perhaps even more so, about whether they can afford retirement.

SMOKE AND MIRRORS

Whatever the situation, most people are victims of "data" circulated by the financial services industry—mutual fund companies, stockbrokerage firms, and banks—which hold that you need at least 70 to 80 percent of your preretirement income in order to retire without becoming a charity case. This estimate has become conventional wisdom and is routinely and endlessly repeated in newspapers and magazines and on radio and television shows that offer financial advice. Little wonder people have come to believe it. It has struck fear into the hearts of baby boomers, who are known for spending, not saving.

There's only one problem: it's not true!

Worse, people in the financial services industry know it's not true. It is clever advertising bait to lure investors.

Money magazine columnist Jean Chatzky has written about a hypothetical twenty-four-year-old earning $35,000 a year and making a 10 percent contribution to his 401(k) plan. She assumes he will face annual inflation of 3 percent, annual salary increases of 6 percent, and investment returns of 8 percent during his working years and 5 percent during his retirement. By age fifty, he'll be making $150,000 a year and have $500,000 in his 401(k). By fifty-nine and a half, when he can withdraw 401(k) money with no penalty, his balance will be $1.24 million.

Chatzky then concludes that he will require $177,650 a year to retire, based on the assumption that he will need 70 percent of his preretirement salary. At this rate, even with Social Security, he will have drained his 401(k) dry by his sixty-ninth birthday! Chatzky's solution: save more and work longer. She says not a word about reducing expenses.

If you sense there is something wrong with this picture, you're right.

SOUL-SEARCHING

Retire on Less Than You Think will clear away the smoke and mirrors from retirement planning and show you that, in fact, you probably can retire much earlier than you thought.

Before you start calculating how much you will need to retire and what sacrifices you must make to do so, you should first do some soul-searching. Decide if you really do want to retire and what you will do with your newfound freedom. Where will you live? What about your friends and social life? People often talk glibly about how much they look forward to retirement, without giving enough thought and planning to the consequences of a major life change that can prove very disturbing and unsettling for those who are not psychologically prepared. Because people are living longer, retirement can stretch on for decades. If you retire at sixty and live to be ninety, you will have spent a third of your life in retirement! That can be a long time if you're just drifting and doing nothing. We all know relatives or acquaintances who retired and found themselves feeling bored and useless. I'm convinced that just such a situation contributed to the death of one of my uncles. After a long, busy career as a civil engineer, he just couldn't cope with lots of unstructured leisure time; for him it was far more stressful than working.

Ilene Cohen is the director of psychology at Bellevue Hospital in

Manhattan and for twelve years was the senior psychologist in the hospital's geriatrics outpatient clinic. She regularly deals with people, especially men, who have difficulty with retirement. Men, she says, are more prone to defining themselves by their careers. "If your sense of power is defined by your job, retirement changes that," she said.

Paul C. Mims, who retired from a life of teaching English and art history in a Philadelphia suburb when he was fifty-eight, had to work through many of these problems on his own. When he retired, his first impression was that he had become invisible. "The minute I announced I was going to retire, it was as if I was no longer there," Mims said. "The same feeling continued for a while after I retired. I was no longer in the loop. That feeling of invisibility lasted until I got a new identity and got involved in a different kind of world." He now devotes more time to painting and does volunteer work at two museums near his home.

Manhattan resident Dan Cuff retired in 1999, when he was sixty-five, after working for nearly thirty years as an editor at the *New York Times*. He expected his wife—a social worker at a high school in the Bronx—would retire within a year or two. But things did not go exactly as he had planned. Because of the effects of a souring economy on the couple's investments, his wife postponed her retirement, leaving Cuff a bit adrift. As a result, he returned to the *Times* on a part-time basis about a year or so into his retirement. He says if he had it to do over again he would have continued working for another five years.

"Retirement seemed like a great idea at the time," he said. "My savings seemed pretty good and I thought my wife would retire soon. It wasn't really a tough decision; I sort of looked forward to it, to a break from getting up and working every day and getting on the subway and all that.

"But in retrospect, it might not have been the right decision. Even though you have a lot of freedom in retirement, you also have to have things to do. To fill up a day sometimes is hard, especially with my wife still working. Some retirees travel all the time, but we can't do that. I have a few things I do, like jogging and messing around on the computer.

"When you're thinking about retirement, you think that if you don't do it you might be dead in two years. But I'm still pretty healthy. I should have just hung in there, I guess."

Working part-time seems to suit him. "I was lucky to be able to do that," he said. "I still have a lot of free time." He and his wife have a house in the Berkshires in Massachusetts, where they go nearly every other weekend. He sometimes stays there by himself for a few days at a time. He says the problems he has had with retirement have been mainly psychological, but he is quick to cite what he calls the "financial component." "Our investments, and the income from them, have shrunk," he said. "It's not debilitating, but you have to think ahead. What if I live twenty more years? Will the money last? I guess it's the same stuff everybody worries about."

COSTS VERSUS BENEFITS

Part of the problem that people like Paul Mims and Dan Cuff encounter may simply lie in the word *retire*. According to my *Random House Webster's College Dictionary*, the first five meanings of the word are: (1) to withdraw or go away to a place of privacy, shelter, or seclusion; (2) to go to bed; (3) to give up or withdraw from an office, occupation, or career, usually because of age; (4) to fall back or retreat, as from battle; and (5) to withdraw from view.

Notice the emphasis on the idea of withdrawing, retreating, or giving up. No wonder retirement is sometimes viewed, and lived, negatively. But that outdated definition in no way describes many current and most future retirees. And it certainly doesn't describe the attitudes of baby boomers, the oldest of whom are facing retirement decisions.

Clearly another term is needed to describe this period of our lives, whether *third age, phase, stage, chapter*, or something else that reflects today's reality. Increasingly, those in this phase aren't about to withdraw, retreat, or give up. More about this later.

The move to this next phase of your life should be based on positive factors, not negatives ones: Retire "to" something rather than "from" something. Retiring simply to flee a situation you don't like can sometimes be an invitation to trouble. On the other hand, retiring in order to have the time and freedom to do something that you have always wanted to do—your second act, so to speak—is highly likely to have a positive outcome. You may even want to continue working, but in a different job or in a field in which you've always been interested but that perhaps didn't pay enough to raise a family or send children to college. Some people may not be able to retire for perfectly valid financial reasons, although I suspect that under closer examination many of these reasons might be greatly diminished.

If you have health problems, for example, and you have no retiree health benefits and aren't eligible for Medicare, you may be forced to keep working until you are sixty-five because of the difficulty and expense of buying an individual health insurance policy. The problem may not be insurmountable and is examined in detail in chapter 6.

If you are caring for an aging parent or parents, that financial burden could cause you to postpone retirement. The same can be true if you have an older child who has moved back home because of financial problems or you are contemplating a divorce that could greatly diminish your assets. Many baby boomers who postponed childbearing may find the expense of sending children to college conflicting with their retirement plans.

Other people, workaholics among them, may never want to retire because they are in love with, or obsessed by, their jobs. Still others have their personal identities tied up with their jobs and can't separate the two, like the men Ilene Cohen mentioned. Then there are those people who continue to work, even if they are unhappy, because they refuse to make even the smallest material sacrifice in order to jump off the labor merry-go-round. A workaholic executive once told a reporter who was interviewing him that he hated the weekends because he couldn't be at the office working. He said he wished he could just go from Friday right to Monday! We all know people who, while not classic workaholics, identify with their jobs so closely that they don't have much of a life outside the office or workplace. This is not a good omen for retirement. Then there's the woman who told me: "I would like to retire, but I won't do it unless I can live exactly as I live now. I don't want to give up anything." She may be missing an opportunity to open new doors and expand her horizons. For people in these situations—or some combination— early retirement may not be the best idea.

However, for most people there comes a time when they want to make a change and move on to another stage of life, much like a caterpillar becomes a butterfly. When that time comes, it is important that you be both flexible and proactive, that you find a way to make it happen. You need to do a costs-benefits analysis. On one side of the ledger are the benefits, mainly freedom and time to fulfill your dreams and desires. On the other side are the costs, mainly a change in lifestyle that will allow you to afford retirement. If the benefits outweigh the costs, go for it!

BACK TO THE FUTURE

First, a little history.

Ken Dychtwald, a well-known gerontologist and speaker who has written numerous age-related books, including (with Joe Flower) *Age Wave: How the Most Important Trend of Our Time Will Change Our Future* (J. P. Tarcher, 1989), likes to remind people that retirement is a very modern concept. "Most of us assume retirement is a given, an entitled period of leisure that's been around forever," he said in the course of several interviews. "That's just not true. In fact, today's retirees are, in many ways, a generation of guinea pigs. They're the first generation of men and women to be living long and retiring young, and attempting to find satisfaction in what has been promoted as this wondrous period, these 'golden years.'"

In fact, he points out, the concept of formal retirement didn't really exist before around 1900. "People weren't craving retirement," he said. "Work was seen not only as a way to provide a living, but a way for people to feel a sense of self-worth. It was an enormously potent engine of socialization, a way for people to stay in touch with other people of all interests and generations.

"Retirement as an institution emerged in the 1920s and really got traction in the 1930s, primarily because of the emerging field of management science and the belief that productivity was the engine that drove capitalism. And productivity, now that we were in a new industrial age, largely had to do with time and motion.

"All the early studies showed that if you were young and strong and quick, you were a valuable piece of the productivity engine. But if you were older and slower, it was a different story. So there was a rising feeling that older people should really be removed from the workforce.

"During the Depression when the unemployment level rose to more than 25 percent, President Roosevelt did a brilliant thing. He created the institution of Social Security whereby two problems could be solved. Older, less productive people could be removed from the workforce—thus boosting productivity—and younger people could be given a shot at a job and a chance to earn a living and start a family."

Although Social Security was signed into law in 1935, the first payments of monthly benefits didn't begin until 1940. The first person to receive a monthly Social Security check was a retired legal secretary, Ida Mae Fuller, of Ludlow, Vermont. Her check was for $22.54. She died in 1975 at the age of one hundred; during her thirty-five years as a beneficiary, she received more than $22,000 in benefits. In 1940, the government paid monthly benefits to 222,488 retirees for a total cost of $35 million. In 2007, nearly 50 million people collected Social Security retirement benefits totaling more than $600 billion.

Those early days of a formal retirement system for workers were very different from what we see now. Even though Social Security benefits were available at 65, the average age of retirement in 1940 was 70. However, the average life expectancy then was 62.9 years—60.8

for men and 65.2 for women. Today the average age for retirement is 62 and the average life expectancy is 78 years—75.2 for men and 80.4 for women. "People back then did not want to retire," Dychtwald said. "They bucked it. Not only did most people not want to retire; most didn't live long enough to do so. Those who did retire only had a few years. Retirement was believed to be a brief period of respite from a life of toil."

What happened to bring us to our current state, in which retirement is seen as another, productive stage of life rather than a short period of rest from life's toil before death? Two factors changed the retirement picture: increased life expectancy and rising affluence. We didn't get to our current situation from the 1930s directly. Social Security benefits were increased by Congress for the first time in 1950, by 77 percent. Between 1950 and 1972, benefits were increased only when Congress enacted special legislation, which it did every few years, usually in response to political pressure. Then in 1972 Congress raised benefits another 22 percent and provided for continuing annual cost-of-living increases linked to the rate of inflation. In the 1960s and 1970s, retirees had more money not only through government programs like Social Security, but from bigger company pensions.

By 1960, the average life span had risen to 69.7 years (66.6 for men and 73.1 for women), and by 1975 it was 72.6 years (68.8 for men and 76.6 for women). It was this two-decade period starting around 1960 that gave rise to the idea of retirement as "golden years" of leisure. "The concept of retirement morphed somewhere around the 1960s and 1970s, the era in which most of us have grown up," Dychtwald said. "We began to glamorize retirement. We began to suggest that retirement, in and of itself, was heaven on earth. Work was the unappealing dimension of life; retirement and leisure were the treasures. Before we knew it, we had people clamoring for retirement. Leisure retirement became a mark of success, and the earlier you retired the more successful you were. If you bumped into people at the airport and they said they were retired at fifty-one, you would believe them to be incredibly successful. That's the era in which many of us have lived. Unfortunately, most people have come to believe that's the standard and that's what everybody should try to do. But that's not what everybody wants to do. And that's not going to make everybody happy in their maturity."

Right now, he and many other experts argue, we are in the midst of another huge, even revolutionary, change in how retirement is viewed. This is in large part because of the 76 million baby boomers who were born between 1946 and 1964 and are starting to leave the workforce. They have remade the face of American life as they have moved through and dominated the demographic pipeline. They are doing the same for retirement. According to various surveys, including one by the AARP, 80 to 85 percent of the boomers plan to continue working, at least part-time, after they retire.

The word *retire*, which went from connoting respite from toil in the 1930s to a life of leisure in the 1960s, is changing again. "Yes, the dictionary says retirement means to withdraw or retreat," Dychtwald said. "But that's not how people are using the word now. We are discarding one model of retirement and embracing another. People see it as a period of engagement, of being involved and pursuing new dreams. There is a sense of self-determination. People now talk about freedom more than security, freedom from the burden of child-rearing and the freedom of being far enough along in their careers to embark on new paths. There is a lot of talk about starting over rather than winding down or retreating. That is a big change. Many people now say, 'Retire is something old people do. I don't have any intention of being old. I'm not going to retire.' Retirement means the end of work, but everybody's talking about wanting to work." Clearly, he added, a new definition of retirement is emerging.

All this, of course, does not mean that people will continue on with the same careers or jobs. It does mean that they view retirement as another career or another job rather than a time of idleness.

It also means that a lot of retirement planners and so-called experts are passing out advice based on an outdated model of retirement.

• • •

Want a look at the "new" retirement? Warning: what you see may change your behavior. A study of retirees by Harris Interactive and Dychtwald has identified four main types of retirees—what they call the "four faces of retirement"—based on experiences, attitudes, and lifestyles. The study was sponsored by AIG SunAmerica, a financial services company that is a subsidiary of American International Group. The survey—which was based on telephone interviews with 1,003 people fifty-five and older—also confirmed that traditional notions of what retirement means are pretty much out the window. "Not only is the meaning of 'retire' changing, even the language of retirement is changing," Dychtwald said. "People no longer talk about not working or taking it easy; they talk about 'reinventing' themselves and 'new beginnings,' of continuing to be productive but on their own terms."

Here are the four categories of retirees found in the survey:

- Ageless Explorers. These retirees represent 27 percent of those surveyed and are the leaders in creating a new definition of retirement. They see themselves in an exciting new phase of life and would rather be too busy than risk being bored. They have the highest level of education and have saved an average of twenty-four years for retirement.
- Comfortably Contents. This group (19 percent) seeks to live the traditional retirement life of leisure; its members aren't as interested in work or contributing to society. They have saved for an average of twenty-three years and spend their time on travel or other recreational activities.
- Live for Todays. These retirees (22 percent) aspire to be Ageless Explorers and may be even more interested in personal growth and reinvention than the actual Ageless Explorers, but they have always focused on the present and didn't devote much time to retirement planning. Having saved for only eighteen years, they have a great deal of anxiety about their finances and are likely to continue working in retirement in order to make ends meet.

- Sick and Tireds. This is the largest (32 percent) of the four groups and its members are in the worst circumstances. They are less educated, have fewer financial resources, and have low expectations for the future. They are more likely to have been forced into retirement by poor health and are less likely to travel, participate in community events, or tap into their potential. They have saved for an average of just sixteen years.

The survey was based on lifestyle and attitude questions, with queries about incomes and net worth added only after the categories were established. "This was not a money-driven study," Dychtwald said. "We weren't looking for who's rich and who's poor. We wanted to know how people are living this segment of their lives. And these four categories rose out of the study like volcanic islands in the Pacific." The study is a strong indicator of the importance of planning for retirement, no matter how much money you make.

Michelle O'Neill, vice president of strategic consulting for Harris Interactive, the parent of the Harris Poll, said that the detailed questions in the survey indicated that "the happiness of people in these categories was not necessarily linked to how much money they had made or had; rather, happiness was linked with feeling financially prepared for whatever retirement lifestyle they wanted."

The study also points to the value of cutting expenses in order to meet retirement goals. Dychtwald noted that the Live for Todays often had made a lot of money and had a lot of good times, but lived beyond their means and didn't plan sufficiently for retirement. "They are financially vulnerable, and that's no fun," he said. "The Sick and Tireds are the largest and most unsettling of the groups," he continued. "Many were dealt a bad hand in that they or someone in their family is ill. They are pessimistic; for many of them, life is a wasteland that holds little promise of security, optimism, hope, or adventure. But some of their problems could have been helped by planning, which they did the least of, despite the fact that their incomes may have been lower or their education less. Long-term-care insurance and more savings would have helped, for instance. It's hard to know which came first. Were they sick and poor and that put them into their present situation? Or were they people who had no vision or dream for the retirement stage of their lives and didn't prepare financially or psychologically?" He added that the Live for Todays and the Sick and Tireds—which make up 54 percent of the total retirees in the study—ought to be a wake-up call for the spend-a-lot-save-a-little baby boomers.

Jay S. Wintrob, the chief executive of AIG SunAmerica, agrees. He called the study a blueprint for future retirees and a "look at what's in store for the boomers." His company, however, didn't help pay for this study for purely altruistic reasons. It will use the survey's results as a tool to help sell its retirement services. Wintrob said he was surprised by the study because of his preconceived notion that the more money you had, the happier you'd be in retirement. "But we found that those who planned the longest were more prepared for retirement," he said, echoing O'Neill of Harris Interactive. "They were happier because their expectations were met."

The study put it this way: "While it would appear that money is the key to satisfaction, the research found that there is a stronger correlation between [satisfaction and] length of time saving and preparing for retirement—regardless of net worth." The study showed, for example, that 75 percent of those with "high financial preparedness" were "extremely satisfied" with retirement. That dropped to 46 percent for those with average preparedness and 26 percent for those with low preparedness. A further breakdown of the data showed that 61 percent of retirees who had saved and planned for retirement for more than twenty-five years were "extremely satisfied." That percentage fell to 51 for those who had saved for fifteen to twenty-four years and to 46 percent for those who had saved for fewer than fifteen years.

Looking even deeper into the results of the study is instructive. For instance, under the category of steps taken to prepare for retirement, 73 percent of Ageless Explorers had contributed to an individual retirement account, or IRA. This percentage fell to 68 percent for Comfortably Contents, 40 percent for Live for Todays, and 24 percent for the Sick and Tireds. As to who had purchased long-term care insurance: Ageless Explorers, 36 percent; Comfortably Contents, 42 percent; Live for Todays, 29 percent; and Sick and Tireds, 21 percent.

As to things they would have changed about preparing for retirement, 49 percent of Ageless Explorers would have started saving earlier, and 45 percent would have saved more; for the Comfortably Contents, the percentages were 54 and 57; Live for Todays, 84 and 79; and Sick and Tireds, 70 and 66. Note that within each group, the percentages are very close for saving earlier and saving more, a further hint of the importance of planning.

"You can have somebody sitting on a pile of $100 million but having a miserable time of it," Dychtwald said. "And you can have a very happy teacher who's been putting aside a hundred dollars a week, who has conceived a dream for retirement that involves, say, some combination of leisure, volunteerism, and work that hits the balance for him or her perfectly. Such a person thought through a plan and gave consideration to the risks and obstacles, and believes the plan can handle them—that was the gem of the whole study. More critical than simply accumulating piles of money is taking time to create a plan. And not just a financial plan but a plan for a new life, for the rest of your life. The plan should be both attractive and doable. Some people dream of plans that are not realistic. It is important to take time over many years to develop a realistic plan and see it work. It is important to think about what you want to do, craft a plan for it, and have the financial elements in place for that plan."

Dychtwald says that an indication of how attitudes toward retirement have changed is that twenty years ago most people would have wanted to be among the Comfortably Contents. "That was yesterday's model: on vacation twelve months of the year," he said. "Now I'll bet most would identify with the Ageless Explorers. People now want more. A life of pure leisure is just not enough—socially, financially, or intellectually." But it takes planning to get there. "It's one thing if you're an Ageless Explorer and want to work because you find it stimulating and fun," Dychtwald said. "It's another if you're bagging groceries because you have to pay the bills."

After establishing the four categories of retirees, the 2002 survey then turned to money. Not surprisingly, those who had planned for retirement the longest had the most money. But answers to survey questions showed that it was a plan and making it work, not the amount of money, that spelled satisfaction.

The Ageless Explorers had an average postretirement household income of $64,800—compared with the overall national average of about $45,000—and an average net worth of $469,800; 75 percent had an investment strategy and a wide range of investments, and 60 percent received assistance in developing investment plans.

The Comfortably Contents' average income was $61,200 and average net worth was $367,500; 68 percent had an investment strategy and a wide range of investments, while 47 percent received assistance with their investment plans.

The Live for Todays had an average income of $46,300 and average net worth was $222,600; 51 percent had an investment strategy and a moderate range of investments, and 38 percent received assistance in developing an investment plan.

The Sick and Tireds' average income was $31,900 and average net worth was $161,200. Only 27 percent had an investment strategy and their range of investments was narrow; just 22 percent received assistance in developing an investment plan.

An important lesson in all this is that becoming an Ageless Explorer is linked more to your state of mind than to your bank account. As this book will show, the group's average household income of $64,800 is not the price of admission. After all, the Ageless Explorers, the Comfortably Contents, and the Live for Todays all have household incomes that exceed the overall national average. For many people, satisfaction stems more from attitude than money. "Statistics on how much you need to retire are very dangerous," Jay Wintrob of AIG SunAmerica said. "Every individual circumstance is different."

Deena Katz, an independent financial adviser and the chairman of Evensky & Katz in Coral Gables, Florida, agrees. "Everybody loves rules of thumb, the press particularly," she said. "But I don't buy those rules of thumb."

THE BABY BOOMERS: THE ELEPHANT IN THE ROOM

Ken Dychtwald's observations that the meaning of retirement is changing and that more and more people refuse to think of themselves as old point to trends that will become very clear as members of the affluent, 76 million–strong baby-boomer generation begin to retire. Boomers are turning fifty at the rate of seven every minute and will continue to do so until 2014, according to *American Demographics* magazine.

Harris Interactive conducted a broad survey for the National Council on the Aging on the "myths and realities of aging." Conducted in 2000, the survey was designed as a follow-up to one done in 1974. The latest study clearly showed an increased feeling of optimism about growing old when compared with the 1974 data. Here are some of the findings:

- 84 percent of the three thousand adults, ages eighteen to eighty, who were surveyed said they would be happy if they lived to be ninety years old.

- 88 percent of those sixty-five and older said that when they looked back on their lives they were generally satisfied.

- 39 percent of the eighteen to eighty group viewed poor health as a very serious problem for older people; in the 1974 survey, it was 51 percent. "The overwhelming message is that Americans have discovered that getting older is not something to fear and that today's seniors are active, vital contributors to society," said a spokesman for Pfizer, which helped pay for the study.

- Nearly half of those sixty-five and older considered themselves to be middle-aged or young. Only 15 percent of people over seventy-five considered themselves "very old."

The survey also showed that retirement is increasingly viewed as a process, not an event—and that work and retirement are no longer mutually exclusive. Good health was considered more important than wealth by wide margins. Despite the general optimism in the survey, there were some concerns: 64 percent of all respondents were worried about losing their memory, and 59 percent were concerned about being denied medical treatments because of age. The effects of these changing attitudes and the approaching tsunami of boomer retirees—along with rising longevity—on our politics and culture will be staggering. "In the twentieth century, we gained an additional thirty years of life," noted Robert N. Butler, president of the International Longevity Center–USA. "It took the preceding fifty centuries to do that. That's extraordinary."

The "Repositioning" Generation

Deena Katz, the financial adviser in Coral Gables, Florida, who is also an associate professor of personal financial planning at Texas Tech University in Lubbock, is a baby boomer in her late fifties with some definite opinions about her generation. She says the fundamental difference between boomers and their parents is in the boomers' philosophy of and approach to "things." "The big issue for baby boomers," she said, "is that they live in the immediate now. They have always given themselves everything they thought they were entitled to. When my folks needed a refrigerator, they saved money and bought it. Notice I said *needed*, not wanted. Now, when boomers *want* a refrigerator, they buy it and pay it off over time. So the boomers are absolutely going to have a hard time making an adjustment to a downsized lifestyle because they haven't saved enough to continue as they have been living."

But many will have to make that adjustment, and she expects the boomers to solve the problem in a way typical of their generation: they will change the rules. "I don't think the boomers will be a generation of traditional retirees," she said. "We will be a generation of repositioning." *Repositioning* is, of course, another way of saying that the boomers are going to continue working in some fashion and staying very active in their version of *retirement*—as has been indicated in most surveys.

But what about this generation's resistance to giving up "things" and living a less expensive life? "They are going to have to make some sacrifices and changes," Katz said. "And that will work for them if they are convinced these changes are positive rather than negative." She also thinks that a lot of boomers and others who say they don't want to move to a less expensive part of the country when they retire will actually do so when the time comes. "We'll see a great exodus from the cities into a simpler, less complicated lifestyle," she said. "But it will be a positive thing for the boomers: not 'You're going to have to sacrifice and downsize!' but 'I want to make my life simpler and the plus in that is that it's going to cost me less.' This will be their salvation from the problem of not having saved enough. When the mutual fund industry says you can't retire on less than seventy percent of your preretirement income, the boomers will say, 'Not me, baby; I'm going to figure it out.' The boomers will give panache to this new life. We're a time-poor generation, and the reward for this coming positive embrace of a simpler lifestyle is time and freedom and money. Saving money is like earning money."

J. Walker Smith, the president of Yankelovich Inc., a consumer research company in Chapel Hill, North Carolina, believes that boomers will do better in retirement than their savings indicate because— despite ups and downs in 2006 and 2007—there have been robust increases in home values over the past two decades. He also thinks the boomers have a special skill. "Juggling debt is a boomer skill, which I don't think a lot of people understand or give boomers credit for," he said. "That ability to juggle debt will probably translate into an ability to juggle resources during retirement to make the most of them." Part of this juggling, he agreed, may likely involve a move to a less expensive area.

So, basically, Katz and Smith think the boomers are going to avoid the train wreck predicted by the mutual fund industry and its 70 percent barrier by simply moving to another track. "All along the boomers have controlled the culture, as they will control retirement," Katz said. "They are redesigning retirement to accommodate what they lack, which is a strong financial base."

A survey by Harris Interactive for Del Webb, the big builder of retirement communities, appears to support Katz's and Smith's observations. In the 2003 survey, 59 percent of baby boomers between the ages of forty-four and fifty-six said they would relocate in retirement; in a similar survey in 1990, only 31 percent of those between forty-eight and fifty-two said they would do so. Of those planning to move, 31 percent expect to end up more than three hours' driving time from their current location. Those who planned to move to another state preferred Florida by 21 percent; Arizona, 18 percent; North Carolina, 10 percent; South Carolina, 10 percent; Tennessee, 9 percent; Colorado, 7 percent; Texas, 7 percent; Virginia, 7 percent; California, 6 percent; and New Mexico, 6 percent.

Where the Money Is

Katz's point that boomers will be active retirees is supported by the results of a survey conducted by Allstate Financial. Among other things, it found that 86 percent of baby boomers plan to spend as much time with activities in retirement as they do with work. About 60 percent think the best years of their lives will come after retirement. Many political observers think the boomers will use their numbers, and the resulting political clout, to force Congress to pass more entitlement programs for the elderly or improve existing ones. Perhaps. But right now the potential influence of these elder boomers is most evident in the advertising business, whether with advertisers who "get it" or those who don't.

Theodore Roszak, the author of *America the Wise: The Longevity*

Revolution and the True Wealth of Nations (Houghton Mifflin, 1998), suggests that corporate America and its media are at war with the Census Bureau. "The young are a vanishing breed," he has written. "The future lies with the old."

 While war may be too strong a metaphor and the young aren't really about to vanish, there is little doubt that the advertising industry has generally been well behind the curve of America's changing demographic landscape. Consider the following facts about this country's older population:

- People over fifty have half the nation's disposable income; 43 percent of new cars are bought by people in this group.
- Those over sixty-five enjoy twice the discretionary income of people twenty-five to thirty-four.
- The total net worth of people over fifty is five times that of other Americans; in the 1990s, the net worth of households headed by people over sixty grew 30 percent—double the national average.
- People over fifty account for 75 percent of the nation's financial assets and 80 percent of its savings and loan accounts.

As the boomers age, these numbers will become even more skewed toward older groups.

So what's going on? Why haven't youth-obsessed advertisers taken a cue from Willie Sutton, the bank robber who said he robbed banks "because that's where the money is." Nothing strikes fear in the heart of a television executive more than learning that one of his or her shows is attracting older viewers. The reason for this fixation on youth may lie in the demographics of the advertising business itself, where many decisions are made by people in their twenties and thirties who have only the vaguest notion of, or interest in, life past fifty. For them, the holy grail of advertising is the eighteen-to-forty-nine age group.

Ann A. Fishman, the president of the Generational-Targeted Marketing Corporation in New Orleans, recalls a meeting she once had at an ad agency in New York. "I was struck by the fact that every person I met except one was young," she said. "But you can't have one age group watching the store. You wind up not being sensitive to the various generational groups."

Gary Onks, an author and consultant who advises corporations on attracting older customers, also faults ad agencies and companies' advertising departments for being made up mainly of people twenty-five to thirty years old who "see only their own plateau." Younger people also forget about the elderly, in part, he said, "because of the increased divorced rates in recent decades and the breakdown of the traditional family, not to mention the mobility of Americans; as a result, a lot of younger people have lost contact with their grandparents and don't know how to bond with older people." He says this myopia about older people will change as seniors become a force that companies cannot ignore without the risk of declining sales. Smart companies, he contends, already recognize this. He often cites Borders bookstores and Cracker Barrel restaurants as examples of senior-friendly companies.

Borders, Onks writes in his book *Sold on Seniors: How You Can Reach and Sell the $20 Trillion Senior Marketplace* (Sold on Seniors Inc., 2001), makes it "so very easy to show up, browse, linger, and socialize: lots of chairs, sofas, helpers, refreshments, room to move about and excellent lighting." He adds: "Their stores simulate warm, cozy dens or family rooms. Seniors love it." Of Cracker Barrel restaurants, he writes: "These places literally ooze every aspect of marketing to seniors. The buildings themselves are designed to look like old country stores. The wide front porches are filled with rocking chairs, just like the front porches homes and stores used to have. The food is down-home, country-style cooking."

But a big problem for companies is that they might not attract aging boomers simply by shifting their products and ads toward an older audience. Remember, the boomers don't think of themselves as old. And they're not the only ones. A lot of current retirees in their sixties and seventies don't either.

Sam Craig, professor of marketing at New York University's Stern School of Business, agrees that there are a lot of untapped opportunities for the senior market. But he contends that mass-market advertisers sometimes appear to ignore seniors not out of ignorance but because of a "basic and subtle dilemma" rooted in the fact that a lot of older people, especially the baby boomers, have a youthful self-image. They don't want to be seen as old. "So if advertisers target the eighteen-to-forty-nine group, they will pick up some older viewers," Craig said. "But if they skew their ads to older viewers, they'll lose the younger ones as well as the older ones who don't see themselves as old. Companies are aware of the demographics, but if they target old they run the risk of being rejected by both groups." He added: "Look at ads specifically directed to older people, like those for vitamins. They don't put people in these ads who are old and decrepit. They pick people who look younger, with gray hair the only real sign of aging. They could be thirty-five year olds with prematurely gray hair."

New York ad executives Marian Salzman and Ira Matathia, coauthors of *Next: Trends for the Near Future* (Overlook Press, 2000), wrote in a report to their clients: "From health care to fashion, businesses will strive to keep up with a graying world. Yet even as the trend continues, those at its center will be doing their best to ignore it: Boomers have already succeeded in renaming their middle age 'middle youth' and are using every tool at their disposal to stave off the inevitable. Smart marketers will play along with this mass delusion." Salzman put it more directly in an interview for my "Seniority" column in the *New York Times*: "The mass delusion of the boomers is that you're never going to grow old, that you will always look as good as you used to look," she said. "You can sell boomers anything if they feel it's going to make them sexy or more desirable."

But what about the dark side of delusion? What will happen to the boomers when they really get old? Will they accept old age as gracefully, say, as the GI generation that survived the Depression and fought World War II? Or will there be an emotional and psychological collision at the junction of Delusion and Reality? Salzman thinks such a collision is a long-term possibility. "But right now delusion is more powerful than the reality," she said. "What we're going to see is people fighting back against the limitations of age in ways we haven't seen before. The boomers will probably figure out a way to make adult diapers sexy."

Ken Dychtwald is troubled by the dark side of the boomer phenomenon and our youth-obsessed culture; his concern is particularly reflected in his book *Age Power: How the 21st Century Will Be Ruled by the New Old* (J. P. Tarcher, 1999). The book sees the aging of the population as a series of financial and social disasters that can be prevented only through measures like postponing the age at which people can collect Social Security benefits and linking payments to the incomes of recipients—so-called means-testing. He also calls for limiting other entitlements, including Medicare, for older people.

Dychtwald said that while he liked to view the future optimistically, the study he did with Harris reinforced some of the negative possibilities he wrote about in *Age Power*. "While the study gives a lot of positive affirmations, I'm troubled by the high percentage of the population for whom old age is not a time of joy and pleasure and freedom, but a time of fear and pain and vulnerability," he said. "And remember, this is a generation that saved and had a lot of benefits—yet half of them are frightened and struggling in retirement. What does this mean for the baby boomers, who aren't going to have some of the benefits current retirees have? The Live for Todays and the Sick and Tireds might well multiply as boomers retire. Our youth-obsessed culture is concerned only with the here and now. We need to wake up to some of these long-term negative possibilities and as a society do more planning and preparing."

Boomers as a Resource

Theodore Roszak is decidedly not pessimistic about the huge numbers of retiring boomers and the graying of America. He, in fact, celebrates it. A history professor at the California State University at Hayward, he is the author of *Longevity Revolution: As Boomers Become Elders* (Berkeley Hills Books, 2001). In this paperback update of his 1998 book *America the Wise*, he contends that the

aging boomers will prove to be one of our culture's richest resources, not a burden. He argues forcefully and convincingly that
the growing number of older people in America is a positive social
development that should be nurtured, not a potential social and fiscal nightmare to be met with draconian measures. He sees opportunity where others see disaster in the Census Bureau projection
that by 2020, people over sixty will make up 25 percent of the
United States population.

Longevity Revolution views the boomers as a great asset, whose
social value will increase as they grow older. This was a generation
that in its youth was energetic and idealistic. He sees its members in
their older years as compassionate and wise. In retirement, they will
have the free time to return to their youthful impulses and devote
themselves to good deeds. Instead of being a burden to their children, he maintains, the boomers will help support their children
monetarily and provide other valuable services like child care.

Roszak is a staunch defender of entitlements for seniors. In
Longevity Revolution he takes a swipe at the mass media, saying that
it has accepted the language of Social Security critics and doomsayers ("demographic time bomb," "on the skids," "giant sponge soak-
ing up so large a share of the federal budget"). He says journalists
often have not checked data with the Social Security Administration, "whose veracity is unquestioned even by anti-entitlement critics." Using relatively modest growth projections, Roszak writes that
the Social Security system will be solvent for at least thirty-plus
years. He argues that if the Social Security payroll tax were to be
raised by about 2 percentage points—half to be paid by employees,
half by employers—the system would remain solvent through the
rest of the century. That seems a modest proposal in a country
whose citizens, as *Longevity Revolution* points out in a chapter on
health care, spend three times as much on casino and lottery gambling as their government does on Medicare.

Roszak writes that the "crisis" in Social Security comes from two
sources: powerful forces on Wall Street that want the business and
stock trading commissions that would be generated from privatiza-

tion of the system, and conservatives who have been hostile to the idea of government social insurance since it was created under the New Deal in 1935. The combination of those forces has proved fairly potent. Part of its success, Roszak argues, is the constant drumbeat of slanted statistics and misleading catchphrases from conservative policy institutes intended to cause panic over Social Security's future. How many times have you heard or read the phrase *looming insolvency* or something similar in discussions of Social Security?

Perhaps as many times as you've heard or read that you need 70 to 80 percent of your preretirement income to retire successfully.

One of the by-products of an aging population is a shrinking pool of younger workers, which can have profound consequences for corporate America. Many companies that once practiced subtle and not-so-subtle age discrimination may soon find themselves fiercely competing to retain older workers. Bill Zinke, a consultant for corporations on hiring and retraining older workers, wants to change the "national mind-set" about older Americans. "The general attitude is that when you reach a certain age, you're over the hill," he said. "You should go somewhere and enjoy the 'golden years.'" Zinke, a former corporate and criminal lawyer in New York, runs his own consulting company, Human Resource Services, in Boulder, Colorado. He is an example of what he preaches: at eighty, he has no plans to retire. "We should not see aging and our increased longevity in a negative light," he said, echoing Theodore Roszak. "Instead of worrying about the graying of America, we should be looking forward to the benefits and opportunities of this demographic change. An older population is also a wiser and more skilled population."

"The Dream Was Always There"

The next time a youth-obsessed advertising agency convenes a focus group to divine how to spend a client's money, maybe Jack

McQuillan should be included. At age sixty-six, McQuillan fulfilled a long-held dream that would have taxed the imagination, drive, and pocketbook of someone half his age. A retired New York City detective sergeant from Staten Island, McQuillan earned a private pilot's license—despite medical problems that might have turned someone less determined to shuffleboard. He had dreamed of that achievement since he was seven. As a boy, McQuillan hung around a small airport on Staten Island, sometimes scraping together $2 for an airplane ride. The airfield has long since been replaced by the Staten Island Mall, but that early love of flying stayed with him through a four-year stint in the marine corps and thirty-four years on the police force. "I was just always too busy working, and my money had to go for raising a family," he said. "But the dream was always there."

Finally, in 1990—nearing retirement and his four children on their own—McQuillan realized his dream and started taking flying lessons at a private flight school in New Jersey. The dream, however, almost ended. Because he is an insulin-dependent diabetic, he could not pass the physical examination required by the Federal Aviation Administration for a private pilot's license. He continued taking lessons for a couple of years because he loved flying so much, although he knew it would not lead to a pilot's license. "I was pretty discouraged," he recalled. He retired in 1996, at age sixty, still harboring dreams of flying.

Then, in 1997, the FAA changed the rules and allowed insulin-dependent diabetics to fly, with certain restrictions and more rigorous and more frequent medical exams. "I was back in the game," he beamed. Since starting lessons in 1990 and resuming them in 1997, he has had successful cataract surgery in both eyes, suffered a broken ankle, and undergone prostate surgery. In 2000, he and his wife moved from Staten Island to Millbrook, New York, in Dutchess County, where he switched to another flight school. His training there was interrupted for a time by restrictions in the aftermath of the September 11, 2001, terrorist attacks on the World Trade Center. But he persevered and was awarded his private pilot's license on August 23, 2002.

For McQuillan, retirement helped fulfill a dream that he had clung to across the decades. "You know how everybody has a dream in which they are flying?" he said. "Well, flying low and slow in a small plane is as close as you can come to that dream in this life." His advice for a successful retirement: "Keep going. Stay active. Don't vegetate."

2

What the Experts Say You Need versus What You Really Need

Remember, You Need 80% of Your Income to Retire!
—SIGN IN A NEW JERSEY BANK

Congratulations! You've made the decision that retirement is for you. You are ready to enter the next phase of your life and pursue other interests and goals. But can you afford it? Unless you're sixty-two, you can't collect Social Security benefits. Do you have enough savings to produce an income stream you can realistically live on? And even if you are sixty-two and eligible for reduced Social Security benefits, there are limits on how much you can earn from working until you reach full retirement age (see chapter 8). That can be important because you may actually want to work, perhaps on a part-time or freelance basis, at something you've always been interested in but never had time for.

PROJECTIONS: REALISTIC AND OTHERWISE

As we work through these questions, the most important thing to remember is to question and be skeptical of most of the so-called ex-

perts, especially those who quote data from the mutual fund and equities industries showing that you need at least 70 percent, and
preferably 80 percent, of your preretirement income in order to retire. These estimates of retirement needs are self-serving, generated
by companies that have a vested interest in convincing people to save
as much as possible—with the mutual funds or brokerage firms, of
course.

Charles Schwab, head of the big discount brokerage firm that
bears his name, writes in his book *You're Fifty—Now What?: Investing for the Second Half of Your Life* (Crown, 2000) that while
the minimum percentage of your income you will need to retire is
70 percent, he is much more comfortable with 80 percent. He even
tries to make the case that sometimes a retired person may need 100
percent—or more!

There have been many magazine and newspaper articles pointing out that Americans are retiring later, reversing a decades-long
trend toward early retirements. These articles are based on surveys, mainly of baby boomers, that show that boomers plan to continue working past the traditional retirement age of sixty-five.
Many of those surveyed cited their meager savings and cutbacks in
company pensions and medical coverage as factors that have led
them to believe that they can't opt out early. But these articles ignore a very important reason that many people think they have to
work longer: the constant drumbeat from the mutual fund and equities industries—and financial writers, planners, and advisers who
rely on their data—that without 70 to 80 percent of their preretirement income, retirees will end up impoverished. (Although
long on inspiration and short on strategy, Lee Eisenberg's book
*The Number: What Do You Need for the Rest of Your Life, and
What Will It Cost?* [Free Press, 2006] at least takes the more realistic approach that everyone's situation and "number" are different
when it comes to retirement.)

All these inflated projections assume, of course, that you make no
changes in your lifestyle or level of expenses when you retire. Well,

before you make any commitments to work longer or resign yourself to a bread line, take a deep breath and consider the advice of Fred E. Waddell.

Waddell, a semiretired money-management specialist in Smith Mountain Lake, Virginia, trains financial counselors. He contends that estimates of how much you need to retire are unrealistically inflated by the mutual fund and equities industries and accuses them of "fear selling" to attract customers and their money. "The mutual fund industry persists in using these inflated figures because they have a vested interest in doing so," said Waddell, who is a retired associate professor from Auburn University in Alabama. "This frightens people into thinking they're going to need a great deal more in savings than they really will. As a result, people oversave for retirement or put off retiring. These unrealistic projections can also be psychologically depressing for a lot of people who think they'll never have quite enough."

The projections are flawed, according to Waddell, because they are based on *preretirement income* rather than on *postretirement expenses*. "Most older people, with their children gone and expenses down, are saving as much as they can in anticipation of retirement," he said. "They may be living on forty percent or less of their disposable income and saving the rest. In my case, I was living on thirty-five to forty percent of my take-home pay, and I think I was typical. Well, when you retire you don't have to save for retirement anymore. So right now I'm living on a hundred percent of my preretirement disposable income, which was only thirty-five to forty percent of my total salary." He continued: "When people say you need X percent of preretirement income, it defies explanation. It's a huge mistake to base these projections on income rather than expenses. The only sensible way is to compare your expenses, preretirement and postretirement. For financial planners to ignore these common-sense considerations raises questions about their objectivity."

Another example of the mutual fund industry's hype that Waddell likes to point out is its tendency to overestimate the future rate of inflation to convince clients that they need to save even more to retire. Estimating future inflation at 4 percent a year rather than a more realistic 3 percent may not sound like a big deal. But remember, the difference between 4 percent and 3 percent is not 1 percent, but 1 *percentage point*. The real difference is 33.3 percent, which means the growth of your future retirement expense is being overstated by one-third!

Waddell says that some financial counselors who work for big firms have telephoned him and, while refusing to give their names, told him he is exactly right on this issue. "They will tell me they can't give their names because they would get in trouble with their firms, where the policies are to rake in as much money as possible with the line that you need seventy to eighty percent of preretirement income to retire," he said.*

Not every expense, however, will decrease when you retire. Waddell points out that if you are not sixty-five, and thus ineligible for Medicare—and your company's retirement plan has no health insurance benefit—your medical expenses may increase, especially if you have to buy health insurance. According to government figures, he said, the average increase for pre-Medicare medical expense for retirees is 125 percent. "A lot of retirees want to travel, so expenses related to that may also increase, but usually only temporarily," he added.

Waddell's advice is wise. But he and others like him are drowned out by the advertising and public relations powers of big mutual funds and brokers. The result is that many Americans have bought into Wall Street's slick sell as they approach the final decade or so of their working lives. Those who started saving late, like many of the estimated 76 million baby boomers who are famous for spending instead of saving, often are convinced that they can't afford early retirement and will have to work much longer than they would like.

---

*In the six years that I wrote the "Seniority" column for the *New York Times*, I from time to time discussed the notion that people didn't need as much to retire as they had been told by stockbrokers and mutual fund salesmen. Whenever I wrote about this, I received scores of letters and e-mail messages from readers agreeing with me and thanking me for pointing it out. I never received a single letter or message from anyone in the financial services industry arguing otherwise.

Some, in a panic, have become born-again savers in an effort to play catch-up, pouring billions of dollars into the mutual funds and stocks that have helped fuel stock market gains since the 1990s. They watch every twitch of the Dow. Their angst is palpable. When the market slumps, they joke about having to work until they are eighty.

Mind you, I am not opposed to saving. More is usually better than less. What I am opposed to is continuing to work when what you really want to do is retire or perhaps change course. This is especially true if you are burned out or in a dead-end job, as many people in their middle to late fifties find themselves. I believe that most people can retire from wage slavery sooner than they think if they are willing to pay a relatively painless price for their freedom: a simpler, downsized life and, perhaps, a move to a less expensive part of the country—and it doesn't have to be remote or far away. This is especially true for those living in expensive, high-tax urban centers on both coasts.

So relax. It can be done, especially if you are willing to make that move to a cheaper location and learn to live within or *slightly beneath* your means. I first began to realize that the mutual fund data were out of kilter when I would travel from the New York City area to visit friends and relatives in the Midwest and South. I was struck by how well they were living on relatively small incomes, at least compared with New York and California. But what if you don't want to move to another part of the country? That's okay. You can still retire on less than you think, especially if you are willing to make a short-distance move. More about this and a simpler life—emphasizing your capacity to focus on the few things that are really important to your freedom and happiness—later. First, the two most important keys to being able to retire on less than you think are your house, which is most people's biggest single asset, and your health insurance.

You need enough equity in your current home to be able to pay cash for a new home in whatever area of the country you choose for retirement; if you elect to stay put, and you are at least sixty-two years old, you may need the equity for a reverse mortgage to boost your income. (Chapter 5 looks at reverse mortgages and the housing issue in depth.)

Because Medicare isn't available until you are sixty-five, you must have health insurance. Don't even think of trying to live without it. One serious illness could put you on the welfare rolls. Only about 30 percent of employers offer any retirement health benefits, so you may have to buy this insurance on your own. Chapter 6 looks at various alternatives available to make sure you're covered until you reach the eligibility age for Medicare.

For working through the numbers at this point, we're going to make the assumptions that you have the necessary home equity and that you are willing to make that move to a cheaper region. The final part of this chapter will deal with those who want to remain in the area where they have always lived.

CRUNCHING SOME NUMBERS

Let's take a hypothetical case and look at the figures.

Joe and Sue Sample are both fifty-nine. They own their own home in an affluent suburb of New York. They have two sons who are grown and living independently. Joe commutes to Manhattan where he is an editor for a chain of medical newsletters; Sue is a teacher at a private school in the town where they live. Their combined income is $150,000 a year. Like many baby boomers, they got serious about saving only twelve years ago, when they began putting the maximum into their company 401(k) plans. They invested mostly in stock funds, and now have a 401(k) nest egg of $400,000. They also have a rainy-day fund of $30,000 in bank certificates of deposit. Joe and Sue would like to retire in six months when they are both sixty, even though they can't collect Social Security until they are sixty-two—and then at a reduced rate. Their Social Security may also be reduced a bit further because, if they retire at sixty, their income will drop during the two years between retirement and age sixty-two. This will somewhat affect the calculation that determines the amount of their monthly Social Security benefits (more on this in chapter 8).

They would like to move to a less congested and warmer area where they can indulge year-round their passion for bicycling. But they don't think they have nearly enough money. They have read that they need 70 to 80 percent of their current income—or $105,000 to $120,000—to retire. Sue has no pension at her job to supplement the savings in her 401(k) plan. Joe has changed jobs several times over the years and has been at his current position for only fourteen years. He will be eligible for a pension plan—in addition to his 401(k) plan—when he is sixty, but will receive only $1,500 a month, or $18,000 a year; if he waits until he is sixty-six (for the couple's age group, the full Social Security retirement age has been raised to sixty-six from sixty-five), his pension will be $1,800 a month, or $21,600 a year. In addition, he will get $200 a month, or $2,400 a year, from a previous employer's pension plan, in which he barely vested. At age sixty, these two income sources will total $1,700 a month, or $20,400 a year. Most financial advisers would probably agree that Joe and Sue could safely take 4 percent a year, or $16,000, from their $400,000 nest egg without fear of using it up while they are still living. This would boost their annual income to $36,400—only a fraction of the $105,000 minimum. Using the nest egg to further increase their income to the $105,000 level would devour the $400,000 in short order.

If they wait until they are sixty-two and can begin collecting combined, and reduced, Social Security benefits of about $2,200 a month, or $26,400 a year, they would have a total income of $62,800—still only slightly more than half of the minimum they have been told they must have. The Samples are worried that they may have to work until they are sixty-six and eligible for full Social Security benefits, which will give them a combined payout of about $3,100 a month, or $37,200 a year. That would lift their total annual income to $79,200, boosted a bit by Joe's bigger pension, which jumps to $1,800 when he hits sixty-six, and by the assumption that their nest egg has grown to $450,000; 4 percent of that gives them $18,000 a year. But the $79,200 is still well shy of the $105,000 mark—which by the way has now grown to almost $118,000, assuming the couple's annual combined income rose 3 percent a year to $168,000.

Now they are afraid they may have to work until they are seventy and delay collecting Social Security until then, when their combined monthly government benefit will have risen to $4,300, or $51,600 a year. Figure 1 shows their income and its sources at various retirement ages.

However, even if Joe and Sue wait until they are seventy, they will still fall short of the mutual fund industry's projection of 70 percent, or $105,000, which actually will have grown to $140,000 assuming their combined salary increases 3 percent a year for ten years, to just under $200,000. The $51,600 from Social Security plus the $24,000 from Joe's two pensions—the first, smaller one was capped when he left the job to which it was linked; the second is capped when he reaches sixty-six—total $75,600. Let's assume, conservatively, that their nest egg has grown to $500,000 by the time they're seventy. The 4 percent annually they can take from that comes to $20,000.

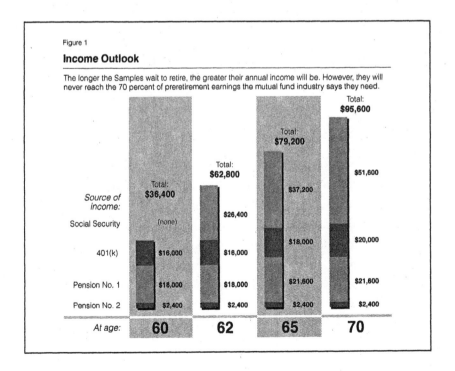

Figure 1

Income Outlook

The longer the Samples wait to retire, the greater their annual income will be. However, they will never reach the 70 percent of preretirement earnings the mutual fund industry says they need.

Source of Income:	At age 60	At age 62	At age 65	At age 70
Total:	$36,400	$62,800	$79,200	$95,600
Social Security	(none)	$26,400	$37,200	$51,600
401(k)	$16,000	$16,000	$18,000	$20,000
Pension No. 1	$18,000	$18,000	$21,600	$21,600
Pension No. 2	$2,400	$2,400	$2,400	$2,400
At age:	60	62	65	70

That still gives them only $95,600 a year—a $9,400 shortfall, compared with the lower $105,000 projection, and a whopping $44,400 gap when compared with the $140,000 projection based on the reasonable expectation of 3 percent annual salary increases. It gets even worse if you use the 80 percent benchmark instead of 70 percent. Just imagine if Joe and Sue bound themselves to Charles Schwab's estimate of 100 percent! They wonder if they will ever be able to retire.

Let's take a closer look at their situation and apply some more realistic projections and estimates to their problem. I have tried to use figures that are as accurate and current as possible. The Social Security benefit estimates, for instance, are based on Social Security Administration data. As a reality check, I found friends whose incomes matched the Samples' and borrowed their Social Security projections—the ones included in periodic mailings from the SSA that tell what you can roughly expect to receive at your full retirement age, as well as sixty-two and seventy. Where I have been forced to make estimates, I have usually based them on my own experiences or the experiences of relatives and friends. Also, while some of the numbers—especially prices—will probably have changed by the time this book is published, the relative differences will likely be very similar. On balance, I think what follows is reasonably accurate.

Location, Location, Location

There are two Web sites, BestPlaces.net and RetirementLiving.com, that help expose the exaggerated estimates of retirement needs by the mutual fund and stock industries. The sites allow you to compare the cost of living among cities around the country, using data from excellent sources, including federal and state governments. (RetirementLiving.com deals more specifically with taxes in the various states. The site's basic services are free, although you can opt to pay a onetime charge of $19.95 for unlimited and forever access to a very useful section called "Great Places to Retire"; there are no charges for BestPlaces.net. Both sites are discussed in greater detail in chapter 4.) BestPlaces.net shows, for instance, that if you make $100,000 a year in New York City, you need to make only $54,802 a year—or about 55 percent of your New York salary—to maintain a *comparable* lifestyle in Jacksonville, Florida. If Tucson, Arizona, is more to your liking, you'll need $59,332, or about 59 percent. Remember, *these comparisons assume you make no changes in your lifestyle*, that you continue to pay a mortgage and continue paying work expenses like commuting, clothes, and lunches. Imagine how much lower these income requirements would be if we eliminated mortgage payments and work expenses. The numbers can go lower still if you trim other spending to achieve a less expensive lifestyle.

Why do members of the mutual fund industry tell you that if you make $100,000, you'll need $70,000 to $80,000 to retire? They want your money. It's that simple.

It's the Expenses, Stupid

Let's apply some of the data from the BestPlaces.net and RetirementLiving.com Web sites and from other sources to Joe and Sue's situation, keeping in mind Fred Waddell's advice to focus on expenses, not income. In addition, let's assume that Joe and Sue would be happy to retire to Tucson, where the climate suits their love of bicycling.

The couple's house is a four-bedroom Dutch colonial. They bought it twelve years ago for $185,000 and spent another $20,000 on repairs and upgrades, including installing a new heating system and rewiring the entire house. They owe $140,000 on their mortgage. Their monthly house payment is $1,000; their property tax is $715 a month, or $8,580 a year, a figure not uncommon in the New York area. Despite a recent real estate slump, since they bought their house there has been a hefty increase in home values in their town, which is within easy commuting distance of midtown Manhattan; if they sold their house today it would likely fetch at least $500,000. After a 6 percent, or $30,000, real estate agent's fee, they could walk away from their house with $330,000. Under current law, that money is tax-free.

The Samples owe $15,000 on a car they bought new last year. Their car payment is $375 a month. They have a second car, which is ten years old and long since paid for. They have another $20,000 of debt in a bank overdraft and various credit card bills. These payments total $500 a month.

The couple's utilities run about $250 a month. In addition, they pay about $170 a month for life insurance and $230 a month for auto insurance—they live in one of the most expensive areas of the nation for car insurance. Their homeowner's insurance, $650 a year, is included in the mortgage payment. Joe's commuting expenses come to $220 a month, and he spends another $150 a month for lunches in Manhattan. Sue takes her lunch to school and walks to work. Together, Joe and Sue estimate they spend $3,600 a year on clothes that they need for their jobs. Their health insurance, provided by Joe's employer, is through an HMO, so they have few out-of-pocket medical expenses.

They spend about $800 a month for food and dining out.

Let's examine these core expenses on a monthly and yearly basis.

	Monthly	Yearly
Mortgage	$1,000	$12,000
Property tax	$715	$8,580
Car payment	$375	$4,500
Credit cards, etc.	$500	$6,000
Utilities	$250	$3,000
Insurance (all)	$400	$4,800
Commuting/lunches	$370	$4,440
Clothes	$300	$3,600
Food/dining out	$800	$9,600
Totals	$4,710	$56,520

Now clearly the Samples have more expenses than those listed above. There are bills for vacations, car maintenance, and home repairs, to name a few. I have not included taxes, other than property taxes, in the calculations so far. But let's use this snapshot of their core, nonvariable expenses in considering their retirement needs.

Imagine they decide to retire to Tucson, where it is almost 41 percent less expensive to live than in New York, according to BestPlaces.net. First they sell their house and pocket the $330,000. They spend $35,000 of that to pay off their car, credit card bills, and bank overdraft. That leaves them with $295,000. They use $5,000 of that to move to Arizona, leaving them with $290,000.

According to BestPlaces.net, housing costs—including taxes and related expenses—in Tucson are slightly below the national average. New York City, partly because expensive Manhattan apartments are included in the calculations, can be more than four times the national average. The New York suburbs, depending on location, can be two to three times the national average. The median price—meaning half are above and half below—of a home in Tucson is $202,400. This compares with about $602,000 in the Samples' suburban New York town and $217,200 nationwide.

Do you see where this is leading?

The Samples can take the $290,000 left from the sale of their house and pay cash for, say, a $210,000 home in Tucson and have $80,000 left to add to the $30,000 they already have in the bank for a rainy day. Suddenly their mortgage payment disappears. Their property taxes drop from $8,580 a year, or $715 a month, to about $1,500 a year, or $125 a month.

Gone are commuting and other work-related expenses. The Arizona state and local income tax works out to 3.9 percent, or $1,950, on a $50,000 income compared to the national average of 5.0 percent. In the New York area, the Samples were paying more than $6,000 in state taxes. In addition, Arizona is one of twenty-six states that does not tax Social Security benefits (see chapter 4).

In Tucson, the couple's food bills will drop by almost one-third. They will need only one car, and their auto insurance—which is much less expensive in Arizona than in the New York area—will drop to $870 a year, or $72.50 a month, from $2,760 a year, or $230 a month.

Suddenly, the $36,400 a year, or $3,033 a month, they will have if they retire at age sixty looks a whole lot better, especially when you realize that they will have no mortgage or rent to pay.

In fact, let's look at what's left of the Samples' estimated core expenses after the hypothetical move to Arizona. The amounts are based on data from various sources, including BestPlaces.net and RetirementLiving.com. The figures for clothing are based on my own estimate using some general cost-of-living data and personal experience. The same goes for food and dining out.

	Monthly	Yearly
Mortgage	$0	$0
Property taxes	$125	$1,500
Car payment	$0	$0
Credit cards, etc.	$0	$0
Utilities	$200	$2,400
Insurance (all)	$338	$4,056
Commuting/lunches	$0	$0
Clothes	$100	$1,200
Food/dining out	$600	$7,200
Totals	$1,363	$16,356

The increased insurance costs represent life insurance premiums of $170 a month, a constant; auto insurance premiums of $72.50 (rounded to $73); $45 a month for homeowner's insurance, which had previously been included in the mortgage payment; and the addition of $50 a month that Joe must pay for company-provided retiree health benefits, which also cover Sue.

Joe and Sue are lucky. His company provides retirees, even those like him who take early retirement after only fifteen years of service, with the same health insurance they had when they were working for the nominal fee of only $50 a month. Still, even if they had been forced to buy health insurance, it would not have broken their budget (see chapter 6).

Remember, the Samples have to live on their current retirement income of $3,033 a month, or $36,400 a year, for only two years. At sixty-two, they can start collecting Social Security benefits of $2,200 a month, or $26,400 a year—bringing their total income then to $62,800. If they find they need more cash during these first two years of retirement, they could cash in one or both of their life insurance policies, which may no longer be such a high priority (see chapter 3). Of course, they could tap into their rainy-day fund, which now stands at $110,000.

The Samples could also take part-time jobs for a couple of years until Social Security kicks in. But when they start to collect Social Security at sixty-two, Joe and Sue will face limitations on how much they can earn without reducing their benefits; at full retirement age, those limitations vanish (see chapter 8).

Joe and Sue should be able to live, and pedal, well within their means in Tucson without having to turn to any of these extra measures.

Portfolios Still Count

Deena Katz, the financial adviser mentioned in chapter 1, agreed that 4 percent was a reasonable amount that the Samples could withdraw each year from their 401(k) plan. But she warned that the $400,000 in their portfolio should be split among several investment choices, including stocks, so that over time their savings are not eaten away by inflation. And she stressed the importance of taking inflation into account when considering returns. "How you take out your money is as important as how you accumulate it," she said. "When people retire, they intuitively want to put all their money into fixed-income investments. That's a mistake. It won't keep up with inflation. Say your money's in a fixed-income fund earning six percent. You take out four percent a year. Inflation is three percent. That means you're losing one percent a year."

at could mean seriously eroded savings when you're older and your need for the money may be more critical.

In the case of Joe and Sue Sample, Katz recommended that they segment their $400,000 portfolio in the following manner:

- 60 percent, or $240,000, in stocks, which have the potential to appreciate in value over time. "Historical data say that sixty percent is likely to allow the portfolio to last the rest of their lives, assuming they keep the modest four percent drawdown amount," she said. However, she added that in the wake of the boom that started in the 1990s, she expected to see lower returns in the next decade or so.
- $32,000 in a money market fund. This is the amount that the Samples want to withdraw over the next two years.
- The remaining $128,000 divided in bond funds with bonds of various maturities of up to ten years.

"Then every year or so," Katz continued, "they should rebalance the portfolio along these lines, using proceeds—when possible—to replenish the money market fund for their two years' worth of withdrawals. Some years there may not be enough proceeds, and they may have to dip into the principal in the bond funds. But other years there will be more than enough from the proceeds and they won't have to touch the principal; the extra proceeds will become part of the principal, keeping their portfolio strong. This way they don't need to sell stock to get money to live on and thus are never forced to sell stock in a down market. The only time they may need to sell stock is when it's gone up."

The Moving Story

Bert Sperling is the chief executive of Fast Forward, the Portland, Oregon, company that runs BestPlaces.net. The site contains figures for 379 metropolitan areas, where Sperling says 75 percent of the population lives. The site also includes data on most other cities and towns regardless of population. The company makes money by selling data to corporations and publications like *Money* magazine that publish "Best Places" articles on where to live or retire. "If people are willing to change their place of living and change their pace of life," Sperling said, "then there are significant savings to be had."

Sperling concedes, however, that many people may not want to retire to less urban areas or be far from their families or where they have spent most of their lives. "We're used to cities, and for some people that's going to be tough to give up," he said. "But the best of both worlds is to move to a small town within an hour or so of one of these metro areas. You have inexpensive small-town living but are still within easy driving distance of the benefits of health care, arts, and culture that cities offer."

RetirementLiving.com. is operated by the Retirement Living Information Center in Redding, Connecticut. It has several categories on retirement living, but the section on state taxes is one of the most useful and popular. The state tax section lays out the facts on each state, but cites no favorites. "We don't make recommendations because of people's different lifestyles and needs," said Tom Wetzel, president of the Retirement Living Information Center. Visitors to the Web site can sign up for a free monthly newsletter via e-mail. Chapter 4 takes a close look at living costs and taxes in various states and regions.

Both Web site operators stress the value of planning. "Retirement is very important," Sperling said. "It's worth a little bit of research and fact-finding."

Now let's assume that Joe and Sue Sample want to retire but don't want to move far from the New York area.

The key to making this work remains the sale of their house and paying off their outstanding bills, just as they did in the hypothetical move to Arizona. In this scenario, they take Sperling's advice and find a smaller, less expensive house, perhaps farther away from New

York City but still in the general region. Western New Jersey and eastern Pennsylvania, for example, offer much less expensive places to live that are within a drive of an hour or so from Manhattan. In fact, the figures for Allentown, Pennsylvania, which is less than a two-hour drive from New York, show that it is considerably less expensive than Tucson. The same is true for Bethlehem, Pennsylvania, which is actually a bit closer to New York than Allentown. Pennsylvania's tax structure is also favorable to retirees.

The closer you get to New York, the higher the numbers go. This could mean that the Samples might have to use some of the $80,000 from the sale of their house that they were able to put in the bank when they moved to Tucson to instead help tide them over for a couple of years until they can collect Social Security. Or they may have to trim their discretionary spending a bit more here and there.

What if the Samples insist on retiring right where they are, in their same house and neighborhood? Well, the hard truth is, they may not be able to do it—not with their big house payment and property tax bill. It could be doable if we change their hypothetical situation and, for instance, assume their home is fully paid for and that they are sixty-two and eligible for Social Security benefits and a reverse mortgage, which could be used to pay property taxes. In their present circumstances, they are probably going to have to relocate. That could mean selling their house and moving to a smaller, less expensive home in the same area—if they can find one. They might have to move to one of those smaller towns with relatively easy access to the more expensive New York area.

But would that be so bad?

I know that many people, in surveys conducted by AARP and others, say that they want to retire right where they are. I wonder if those surveyed would answer the same way if the question explained that in order to do that they might have to delay their retirement by three, five, seven, or ten years and have much less discretionary income than if they moved to a less expensive place? Is driving an hour or two to visit family and friends so difficult? Might it be worth it if you could retire earlier and in greater financial comfort? And if you're moving to another area of the country, you're never more than a few hours away by plane; you can always pick a spot with easy access to a major airport hub, which usually means cheaper flights.

Moving to a new place can be an adventure, a chance to meet new friends and have new experiences. Don't reject it out of hand.

Consider David and Anita Kimery.

In 2005, when he was sixty-six and she was fifty-seven, the Kimerys retired from Chicago to Oxford, Mississippi. Because they were looking for a college town so David could complete his undergraduate degree, the two had considered Chapel Hill, North Carolina, and Athens, Georgia. A native of Oklahoma, he had worked as a computer systems programming consultant for an insurance company; Anita was a human resources specialist.

Since 1993, the town of Oxford and Lafayette County in northern Mississippi have successfully lured retirees to the area, helped in large part by the presence of the University of Mississippi. Christy Knapp, director of the Retiree Attraction Program sponsored by the Oxford-Lafayette County Economic Development Foundation, said that so far the program had attracted more than six hundred retiree households to the town of 18,000 and the surrounding area. "These are people who have moved here permanently and bought homes," Knapp said. According to BestPlaces.net, the median price of a home in Oxford is $163,000.

"We just love the atmosphere in Oxford," Anita said. "We wanted a slow pace. Plus, the people are really friendly. Oxford is a lot different than Chicago, but we had no trouble adjusting to southern culture. I had lived in the South for a short period when I was young, so I kind of knew what to expect."

David, a full-time mathematics major at the University of Mississippi, added, "We're here for the long haul." Both cited the fact that housing, taxes, and insurance costs are much less than in Chicago.

Whatever you do, the most important element is having a home that is paid for or has enough equity, as in the case of the Samples, to allow you to sell it and buy another, less expensive home free and clear or to tap into your current home's equity through a reverse mortgage if you are sixty-two. This is the key that unlocks the possibility of retiring early for most people.

Your personal situation may be similar to that of Joe and Sue Sample, or it may be very different. Chapter 9 contains worksheets so that you can figure out your own road to retiring early on less than you think.

It can be done. And the reward for doing it is freedom.

SOME IMPORTANT LESSONS

If you're still doubtful, let's take a look at two real-life examples of people who have successfully retired on much less than the experts said they could and have refocused their lives in ways that are more meaningful to them. While you may not want to live exactly as they do, their experiences can teach us some important lessons.

"The Happiest Guy in Texas"

I call Elton Pasea a mutual fund salesman's worst nightmare. I interviewed Pasea, a native of Trinidad, in 1998—when he was seventy-six years old—for my first "Seniority" column in the *New York Times*. At that time, he was living quite nicely in Nederland, Texas, on $1,200 a month: $700 from Social Security and $500 from a union pension.

Very little has changed in his circumstances since then. By 2007, when he was eighty-five, his monthly Social Security check had increased to $875, raising his total income to $1,375 a month, or $16,500 a year. "I'm loaded now," he said. "I'm having the time of my life." He owns his own home and has about $21,000—his life's savings—invested in bank certificates of deposit. He has never owned stocks, bonds, or mutual funds. "I don't know anything about stocks," said Pasea, a widower. "I've never even considered them."

He apparently has never considered that, according to projections by mutual fund companies, he should be eating cat food—or at least wallowing in financial misery, sorry that he didn't take the companies' advice and save more. He doesn't have a million-dollar nest egg, and his income isn't at least 70 percent of his preretirement figure that the projections say he needs. How can the poor wretch possibly be having a good time? The reality is that the Elton Paseas of this world are living proof that many such estimates of retirement needs are self-serving, designed to entice people to pour money into mutual funds and stocks.

Pasea retired to Nederland on the Gulf Coast in 1984 after forty-one years of roaming the world as a merchant seaman. He wanted a small town and a warm climate in which to indulge his lifelong passion: bicycling. He rides every day and racks up about four thousand miles a year. He takes a couple of big bicycle trips a year—one of them usually in Europe—all within his annual income of $16,500. On his overseas bicycle trips he often saves money by staying in youth hostels.

He doesn't have many health-related expenses. Wiry and fit from all that riding, he also watches his diet, which consists mostly of fish and vegetables, and he has never smoked.

Pasea's modest house is paid for. If it needs repairs, he usually does them himself. Texas has no state income tax, and his property taxes run about $400 a year. His utility bills average $100 a month. Until 2004, he drove a 1984 Nissan with "only" about 250,000 miles on the odometer; in 2004 he replaced the Nissan with a four-year-old Ford Focus.

In 1998, he was often living on less than $500 a month and using the rest for travel or savings. Now, he says, he is less concerned about saving. "But it's difficult for me to spend thirteen hundred and seventy-five dollars a month," he said. "It takes very little for me to live." However, he does not stint when it comes to bicycles. He has spent about $3,000 on his two high-performance road bikes and related equipment. Music is another passion. An amateur musician who used to play the clarinet, Pasea sometimes splurges on

CDs—modern classical (his "first love") and jazz. And the reward of such a spartan life? "I'm the happiest guy in Texas," Pasea said.

"A Meaningful Life"

In 1987, at the age of fifty-five, James McCain retired early from a teaching career at a university where he was an associate professor of American studies. He did so in order to have the time to complete a book on the history of ranching in the Southwest that he had begun four years earlier.

In 1990 he and his wife moved to a small town in New Mexico, where she had been hired as a public health nurse. He continued his research and writing and they subsequently bought a modest bungalow on six acres close to a national forest area. This gave them the space they needed to keep horses they both loved.

They paid $50,000 down from the sale of their former house on the new $65,000 property and took out a mortgage for the remaining $15,000. With McCain's reduced retirement income of less than $1,000 a month, along with his wife's nursing salary, the two lived quite comfortably.

The ranching book was published in 1993. It was his third book. While teaching at the university, he had published another history and a biography. The ranching book, never intended as a best seller, received superior reviews from academic historians.

But the next year McCain and his wife divorced. In the settlement, she took all the couple's savings—$30,000—and he got the house and the mortgage. Suddenly McCain was faced with having to maintain himself, the house, and a substantial piece of property with considerably less money than he had anticipated. As he put it, "Our investment here was a two-income proposition, and now I was stuck with the investment and one income." But he had a keen sense of what he wanted: freedom and the independence to live and work on his on terms, and he was willing to make sacrifices for that kind of life.

His response should be instructive to all those who think they can't afford to retire. "I could have gone back to work or taken a part-time job at Wal-Mart or McDonald's," he said. "I did work part-time for a while. But working for someone else was truly a waste of my time." Instead, he organized his life and finances in such a way that he is able to live within his modest income, although he concedes that he usually "lives along the edge." He calls himself an "edgemaster." Nevertheless, his life is not without cultural comforts. He drives to El Paso for classical concerts and is active in the literary life of the Southwest.

He has no expectations of making money from his books. "When I quit teaching to finish the ranching book, it was not primarily a financial decision," he said. "My research for the ranch history was all archival work, and it took a lot of travel to get to the sources. I couldn't do it while teaching full-time. Survival was important, sure, but money wasn't."

His lifestyle is not for everyone. For instance, he continued to keep two horses while driving a 1977 Volkswagen Beetle with a twice-rebuilt engine and 400,000 on the odometer. He uses a 1959 Chevrolet pickup, which he bought for $450 in 1974, to pull his horse trailer and to haul wood for his stove and feed for the horses.

Most of his monthly income is from two sources: his university pension, now $1,125, and a Social Security check for about $952. This gives him an annual income of $24,924. In addition, he usually makes a few hundred dollars a year from writing.

Like Elton Pasea, McCain owns no stocks or bonds. He used to have a small stock portfolio, but its value declined dramatically in the market crash of 1987. He then got out of stocks altogether, realizing that he didn't have the temperament for the market's ups and downs nor the interest in learning how to manage stock investments. His father and his grandfather, both economic victims of the Great Depression, had taught him that stock investments were risky.

In 1999, he had used most of his savings to pay off the $9,000 that remained on his home mortgage. At one point in 2002, he had just $7,000 in a savings account at a local bank and had to use al-most $5,000 of it to buy a 1995 Volkswagen Golf to replace his vin-tage Beetle, which he sold for $2,455. He later took out a reverse mortgage on his home and six acres to buy an adjoining six acres, giving him a total of twelve acres. He estimates the value of his house and expanded property at about $300,000, although the reverse-mortgage debt for the additional six acres is approximately $80,000. He has since rebuilt his savings account to $22,000.

His core monthly expenses are minimal: $125 for utilities; $106 for a Medigap health insurance policy; $350 for food; $100 for homeowner and auto insurance; $63 for property taxes; and $150 to maintain and feed his two horses. Because he is a Korean War vet-eran and his income is below a certain level, he is able to get pre-scription medicines through the Veterans Administration for a small co-pay. "But I have to spend a good bit to maintain this place and my car and truck," he said. "I have to be prepared for things breaking down. For instance, I recently had to buy a $400 pressure tank for my well and had to reshingle my house. I cut corners everywhere I can. I usually car camp when I travel, which is easy to do in the West. I rarely eat out. If I want to buy something I have to save the money for it. I can't afford payments and interest. But I'm unable to save on a regular basis; at the end of the month if I can stick $100 in savings, I do. I've made sacrifices in order to have the freedom to fo-cus on the very few things I most like, the things that give me a re-ally meaningful life."

McCain, now in his late seventies, has published a revised paper-back edition of his ranch history, as well as another book, an account of Santa Fe before the Civil War. He is at work on a biography of Kit Carson. His books are truly a labor of love. Although highly re-garded, none has ever recovered even the expense of the research and writing. "I write things that need to be written," he said, "not things in order to sell. It might be nice to sell loads of books, but that's not my real purpose. I have a low income compared with oth-ers in my age group with my education and experience. I have given up things that most people wouldn't think of giving up, like expensive trips, fancy cars, and RVs. But I manage to live pretty well. I'm blessed in being able to live the life of a rich man without a rich man's income." He figures that in a pinch, he could sell lots off his twelve acres as home sites. But he calls that a last resort. He doesn't want to risk noisy neighbors. Sitting on his porch in the late evening, under the clear, star-filled New Mexico sky and looking at the mountains, it's easy to understand why.

Despite his limited income, McCain says he has thrived in "retirement" because he has an "old-time attitude." "I grew up in the Great Depression," he said. "My philosophy is to 'make do.' I drive an old car and truck, and I repair things instead of buying new. You've got to be willing to darn your own socks and shoe your own horses. That's a reality for me, but it's also a metaphor for the price of my freedom. That's the way I've chosen to live in order to have the freedom I desire. And, by the way, I take pride in being able to shoe my horses. Not many men at my age still do that. But to do what I do you probably have to live in a part of the country where property prices and taxes are lower. It'd be impossible to live as well as I do—to live on twelve acres with two horses, not to mention a whole national forest and two great wilderness areas out my back door—on my income in northern New Jersey, for example."

What this all really boils down to, he repeats, is living a meaningful life as you define it. "There are two ways to live at my age," he said. "You can have financial security or you can have a meaningful life. A combination of both, in my experience, is rare. Many financially secure people I meet are not leading meaningful lives—they are looking for distractions and external meaning. They spend a lot of time rattling around or watching TV."

He said that many of these people have spent years building the financial security they've been told by brokers and mutual fund salesmen that they must have to retire. Then they retire and often don't know what to do with themselves. They may not be happy or find their lives very meaningful, despite their money. "Financial security is a new concept in human history. It's great, but it has its blind side that brokers don't tell you about. It doesn't necessarily lead to a meaningful life, and it can collapse very quickly, as my father and grandfather taught me. An illness, a divorce, a stock market meltdown—any of those could wipe it out overnight. And if you aren't leading a meaningful life and your financial security disappears, what do you have left? Truly blessed are the people with meaningful lives. Add financial security and you're blessed even more. But that's damn rare!"

3

Cutting Back and Simplifying Your Life

Any kind of debt has to be looked at as a mortgage of future income.
— DR. FRED WADDELL, MONEY-MANAGEMENT SPECIALIST

Many of us yearn for a simpler life, with fewer responsibilities and possessions. Such a change can be psychologically liberating; it can also be an important element in reducing your expenses and allowing you to retire early and on less than you believed possible.

Always remember: *cutting expenses increases income.* That may sound simplistic, but consider how many people ignore it. They worry about how to get more money in the form of a raise or an extra job when, in fact, they can often accomplish the same goal just by cutting expenses. You can, in effect, give yourself a raise.

DRAWING THE LINE

Ron and Barb Hofmeister are paragons of simplification. For fourteen years, from 1989 until 2003, they lived full-time on the road in a recreational vehicle. "Everything we own is with us on the road," Barb Hofmeister said from her cell phone somewhere in Minnesota during their road days. "We loved it from the beginning. There was such a sense of freedom, a sense of adventure. It simplified life so much."

In 1989, two weeks after Ron Hofmeister, then fifty-six, retired as deputy director of finance for the Michigan Department of Transportation, the couple allowed the lease on their Lansing town house to expire, put most of their possessions in storage, and hit the road. Three years later they sold what they had in storage and never looked back. They started out in a twenty-four-foot motor home and finally graduated to a $200,000, forty-foot diesel-powered model. The Hofmeisters have written three books about their mobile life, including *Movin' On: Living and Traveling Full Time in a Recreational Vehicle* (R & B Publications, 1999). They also have a Web site (www.movinon.net) that, like the book, offers practical advice for those interested in their alternative lifestyle.

Ron Hofmeister said that their diesel motor home got ten miles a gallon, but that they drove it only seven to ten thousand miles a year. They towed a small Toyota pickup and two bicycles for local travel. They got their mail through a mail-forwarding service in Livingston, Texas. They also "domiciled" in Texas, using the address of the mail service, so that's where they voted and maintained driver's licenses while on the move. Barb Hofmeister said they had not had any trouble getting medical care on the road. "In fact, we've both had major surgery on the road," she added. The longest they stayed in one place was seven months. Usually they traveled two hundred miles and stayed for a week. "We loved this life," she said. "We followed the sun and enjoyed the best weather all year."

In 2003, the Hofmeisters sold their motor home and were able to buy an affordable house in Arizona. "We had planned to buy a smaller RV and return to the road as part-timers," Barb said. "But with gas prices what they are, we've been doing other kinds of travel." Still, the "road lifestyle" has become a way of life. For the Hofmeisters, simplicity and lower expenses are the most important things.

Too Much Stuff

Most people probably don't want to go as far as the Hofmeisters in simplifying their lives. The couple's experience is intended as a starting point for thinking about what you really need in your life. While it's true that we are in some ways defined by our possessions, and there are certain things we would not and should not cast aside, most of us are simply way over the top in this department.

My wife and I have no children. We live in a three-level, four-bedroom house in Manhattan, Kansas. We have two cars, two televisions, three sets of dishes, six regular telephones, two cellular phones, and three computers—and a garage, basement, and storage rooms filled with stuff we haven't looked at or used in years. An exercise machine serves as a coat rack. We have thousands of photographs and slides, many of which are duplicates of the same people or scenes. We still have our decades-old college textbooks, as well as hundreds of books I have squirreled away under the pretense that I'll read them someday.

You get the picture.

Clearly we are candidates for a garage sale. So are many other people who are considering retirement. I look forward to eliminating much of this clutter from my life. I might start collecting it again, but at least I will have made a fresh start.

The three most important things to remember are simplify, simplify, simplify. If retirement is a new beginning, let it be so—free of unnecessary baggage from the past. You will feel lighter and your wallet will be heavier.

Take your house.

As chapter 5 will show in detail, for most people their home is their most valuable asset and one of the main keys to retiring sooner and on less money than they thought possible.

Value aside, do you really want or need to retire in a home that is probably much bigger, and more difficult and expensive to maintain, than one or two people need? Moving to a smaller house, whether nearby or farther away, not only frees up the money in your current home but may well free you from a lot of yard work and other home maintenance and worries. There'll probably still be room for children and grandchildren to visit. If not, there are always motels and hotels. After all, you can't be expected to maintain a big, expensive house just so that relatives will have a place to stay a few nights a year.

Whether you plan to buy an existing home or build a new home, be realistic about how much space one or two people really need. Remember, your goal is to cut some corners so you can retire early. Moving from a four- or five-bedroom house to one with two or three bedrooms is a relatively painless corner to cut.

The True Cost of a Car

If you're serious about trimming back on things, you need to take a hard look at your car or cars. They are a money pit.

First, you'll probably be able to reduce your transportation needs to one car. Not only do you eliminate a car or lease payment, or free up some money if you paid cash, but you also greatly reduce your auto insurance bills, which in some states—like New Jersey, where I lived for many years—are considerable.

What will that one car be? Unless there are special tax issues involved, the most expensive thing you can do is buy or lease a new car every two or three years. The least expensive route is to purchase a used car. There is also a middle way: buy a new car and run it until it dies.

One of the problems with a new car is that its rate of depreciation, or decline in value, is much higher during the early life of the vehicle. Buying a used car, or keeping a new car for a long time, allows you to avoid much of that depreciation or minimize it by spreading it out over many years, perhaps ten to twelve. However, a plus to getting a new car every two or three years is that repair costs are reduced because your car is always under warranty.

If you want a demonstration of how really expensive a car is, go to the Edmunds.com site on the Web. Click on the "True Cost to Own," or "TCO," section. There you'll be able to select a car and see the estimated costs of ownership for five years.

Take for instance a 2007 Chevrolet Malibu four-door sedan with a 3.5-liter six-cylinder engine. According to Edmunds, the estimated new-car purchase price in New Jersey would be $20,330, including that state's sales tax and fees totaling $1,419. The price of the car without the taxes and fees is $18,911, a number that will be useful in some later calculations.

The total cost of owning that Malibu for five years—the TCO—would be $40,087. That includes depreciation, financing, insurance, taxes and fees, fuel, maintenance, and repairs. That works out to an average per-mile cost of 53 cents over the five-year period. (The Internal Revenue Service, however, allows you to deduct only 48.5 cents a mile when the use of your car is a tax-deductible business expense; many companies use the IRS figure to reimburse employees who use their cars for company business.)

Let's look more closely at four of the expense elements in the Edmunds calculations: depreciation, financing, maintenance, and repairs.

Depreciation is the amount by which a car declines in value from its purchase price. As we'll see, most depreciation takes place early on, especially during the first year. In calculating depreciation and resale values, Edmunds assumes that you will drive the car fifteen thousand miles a year, keep it in "clean" condition, and sell it to a private party. If you sell the car to a dealer or use it as a trade-in, its value would probably be lower.

Financing is the interest expense on a car loan. The amounts for the Chevrolet Malibu in figure 2 are for someone with a good credit rating and assume a down payment of 10 percent and a loan term of sixty months. Edmunds is able to constantly update its Web site to account for the slightest changes in interest rates for loans—and fuel prices—which I obviously can't do here. If you go to the Edmunds Web site you will get a different number for interest charges, fuel costs, and the True Cost to Own, depending on current rates and prices. Financing charges are typically based on the balance due and will decrease over the five years as that balance declines.

Figure 2

Costs of Owning a Typical New Car

Some costs, like maintenance and repair, rise as a car gets older. Others, like depreciation and taxes, are much higher when a car is new. Assuming steady use and a clean driving record, fuel and insurance costs rise gradually with inflation.

	First year	Second year	Third year	Fourth year	Fifth year	Total over five years
Depreciation	$ 7,392	$ 1,896	$ 1,668	$ 1,479	$ 1,327	$ 13,762
Repairs	0	0	96	226	329	651
Maintenance	353	541	440	1,004	1,148	3,486
Taxes and fees	1,419	391	328	285	243	2,666
Financing	1,309	1,057	786	494	179	3,825
Insurance	1,136	1,176	1,217	1,235	1,304	6,068
Fuel	1,814	1,868	1,924	1,982	2,041	9,629
Total	$ 13,423	$ 6,929	$ 6,459	$ 6,705	$ 6,571	$ 40,087

Source: Edmunds.com; data for a 2007 Chevrolet Malibu with a 3.5-litre engine.

Maintenance includes work that needs to be done to your car on a regular basis, like oil changes. It also includes unscheduled things like replacing batteries, brakes, hoses, mufflers, lights, and so on.

Repairs refer to work that must be done on your car but is not covered by the manufacturer's warranty.

Both maintenance and repairs—as you might expect—will increase as your car ages.

Putting all the cost elements together, figure 2 shows how Edmunds comes up with the $40,087 that it costs to own a $20,330 car.

As you can see, and probably already know from experience, depreciation is the killer. The value of the Malibu drops by $7,392 the first year you own it. But in the fifth year, its value will drop by only $1,327. While it's true that maintenance and repairs will rise as a car ages and depreciation drops, as you can see in figure 2 it's not an even match—not even close.

Now imagine that instead of buying that Malibu new, you buy it when it is three years old. Edmunds estimates its resale value then at $7,955 (the purchase price of the car, without sales tax, minus depreciation). It would have only 45,000 miles on it and the bulk of its depreciation would be in the past, greatly decreasing its per-mile costs. If the car were five years old, with 75,000 miles on it, you could pick it up for $5,149. By then, depreciation would have tapered way off and the per-mile costs would be even less. Most modern cars can easily go 100,000 miles or more without serious mechanical problems. If you buy the car with 75,000 miles on it, you can reasonably expect to drive it another 30,000 miles, or two years, without a serious breakdown. Now look back at figure 2. The price of the five-year-old car—$5,149—that you're going to drive for two years, or perhaps longer, *is $4,139 less than the depreciation alone on a new Malibu for just the first two years!*

If you drive that five-year-old car longer than two years, the per-mile cost gets less and less the longer you drive it—to a point. That point is when repairs get too expensive. More about that later.

I have some friends who are very good at buying used cars. They often wind up with some very fancy automobiles—ten-year-old BMWs and the like—for less than the price of a new subcompact.

Because I have never been very skillful or lucky at buying used cars, I have adopted the middle way: buying a new car and running it as long as possible. While you will take the initial hit on depreciation, keeping the car long enough—ten years or so—will spread the loss over enough years so that it is much less painful than buying a new car every three years or so. Remember, most of the depreciation occurs in the first three years—and especially the first year—of owning a new car. Note that the five-year depreciation total on a new Malibu is $13,762, with the drop in the fifth year being only $1,327. That averages out to a bit over $2,752 a year. If you keep the car for ten years—and even assume that at that point it's worth zero—the per-year average drops to $1,891. If you keep it twelve years, that average declines to $1,576. By keeping the car twelve years instead of three, you cut the average annual depreciation to $1,576 from $3,652.

Back to repairs. They will climb as a car gets older. The trick is to know when to stop—in terms of both expense and inconvenience.

In 1991, I bought a new Saab 900 and drove it for eleven years, putting close to 150,000 miles on its odometer. The price of the car, without sales tax, was $18,300. My per-year depreciation cost worked out to $1,663. Actually, it was less than that, but for our purposes I'm assuming that the value of the car was zero at the end.

During the last three years that I owned the car, I had to have some repair work done, but it never ran more than $1,500 a year. Each time I had a $500 or $600 repair bill, I would remind myself that this amount was less than just two monthly car payments on a new car. Finally, however, the Saab needed some extensive transmission work that was going to cost several thousand dollars. Plus, the frequency of repairs was becoming an inconvenience. I decided it was time to get rid of the car, which I donated to a charity in exchange for a tax deduction. My decision was not the result of any magic formula, just my own sense of timing based on expense and inconvenience.

Jeff Brown is a freelance writer and former personal finance columnist for the *Philadelphia Inquirer.* He admits to having a bee in his bonnet on the subject of cars and how much they cost. In his column, he has complained that "too many people buy new cars to keep up with the Joneses," adding that "over a lifetime of car ownership, the cost can be enormous—forcing many serial new-car buyers to delay retirement for years."

He expanded on this in an interview. "An awful lot of our car culture is based on the idea of showing off with a fancy and expensive new car," he said. "If that really, really matters to you and is part of what makes you happy, I guess you've got to spend money for it." Otherwise, he advocates buying a used car or keeping a new one for as long as possible. "While I don't think you should live a life of want and be miserable or inconvenienced, I do think you ought to look very closely at value and what really matters to you," he continued. "It's wonderful to have a new Mercedes, but I wouldn't get pleasure from it worth the additional ten or twenty thousand dollars it would cost. Especially as you get older and are perhaps looking to retire and fulfill a dream. If instead of a Mercedes you bought a used car, it could mean retiring earlier and easier. And you'd still be driving a decent car. I'm not talking about driving an old beater down the road trailing smoke and parts. There are some awfully good used cars out there, like those that have just come off lease. I'm talking about a car that still has eighty percent of its life in it, but has lost fifty to sixty percent of its cost. It's value, a good deal."

For those who want to keep a car until it dies, he stresses the importance of regular maintenance: "The trick really is good maintenance. Cars are so much better made now than they used to be. Sure, repairs increase as a car gets older, but a car that's been fairly well maintained ought to run to a hundred thousand miles before it needs major repairs." He says he considers a major repair something that requires work "deep in the heart of a transmission or engine and involves things like pistons or crankshafts. If you have to replace things that hang on the outside of the engine—alternators and pumps, for instance—to me those are maintenance items like tires and brakes. But a major repair is a serious issue and may be the point at which you decide it's no longer worth it. My rule of thumb is that when the annual maintenance costs get close to what the payments would be on a new car, then you're probably paying too much for maintenance and it might be time for a new car. But short of that it's just a matter of comparing what it costs to maintain and what it costs to buy new. Of course, you have to factor in the headache value of putting up with possible breakdowns and inconvenience."

There is yet another school of thought on cars that recommends making major repairs—even if they are expensive—and getting a second or third life out of a vehicle. This is probably best exemplified by James McCain, the retired professor in chapter 2. His Volkswagen Beetle had a twice-rebuilt engine and 400,000 miles on the odometer before he finally sold it.

Although admittedly not for everyone, this method of coping with transportation is not without its merits. Suppose you spend, say, $5,000 to $7,000 to rebuild a car's engine and transmission plus other items that may need more than routine maintenance. That's pretty cheap compared to the $20,000 you would spend for a new car. The rebuilt one might run nearly as long as the new one before needing major work.

Wherever you come down on the car issue, there's no argument that cars are an expensive, if necessary, component of our modern life. The most expensive way of all is to lease or buy a new car every two or three years. If that's been your practice, it's a great place to start cutting expenses so you can retire on less than the "experts" say.

It's Only a Dollar

One of my pet peeves about money is how fast the little things can add up. Perhaps during your workweek you buy a couple of cans of cola or bottles of water a day from a machine or a deli that charges $1 each for them. That's $10 a week, or $520 a year. If you buy a case of water or soda from a discount store, the per-item price drops to about 25 cents. Stick a couple of bottles or cans in your bag or brief-case and save $1.50 a day, or $7.50 a week—or $390 a year.

Let's take this a step further. If you took that $7.50 a week, put it aside, and each month put the $30 you would have accumulated into some type of savings or investment earning 6.5 percent, in ten years you would have more than $5,000. In twenty years, you would have more than $14,000! And you haven't given up anything.

Do you spend $10 a day on lunch? Bring your lunch for a cost, say, of $2 and save the $8 difference. That's $40 a week you could invest. In ten years you would be almost $27,000 richer; in twenty years, almost $77,000! Again, you haven't given up anything. In fact, you may have gained in the health department because the food you bring from home is likely to be better for you than what you buy in a restaurant or over a lunch counter.

You can also look at this as money you don't have to spend when you're retired. Or, if for you retirement means continuing to work on your own terms or at something you've always dreamed of, just cutting back on expenses for lunch and drinks either before or after you "retire" can make your goal that much more possible.

These calculations don't take inflation or taxes into account, but the point is clear and you should think about it the next time you casually drop a few bucks on something you could get cheaper elsewhere or easily do without.

Lotteries are another pet peeve. Sure, there's no harm buying a $1 lottery ticket now and then when the jackpot gets huge. But I used to work with a man who every week would spend $30 on lottery tickets. He used to laugh when I pointed out that the odds of winning a state lottery were astronomical. "Well, somebody has to win," he would shrug. I finally got his attention when I pointed out that if he invested that $30 a week, or $120 a month, for thirty years at 6.5 percent interest, he would have almost $130,000. He said he had a friend who spent $100 a week on lottery tickets. Well, $400 a month for thirty years at 6.5 percent would come to more than $425,000! My workmate was astounded. I don't know if he stopped playing the lottery, but I'm sure these calculations were in the back of his mind every time he bought a ticket.

The Whopper Test

Jeff Brown, the former *Philadelphia Inquirer* columnist, looked at the issue of spending from another angle. In one of his columns, he asked if you would be so quick to buy a can of Coke from a machine if, instead of $1, the price was $5. That's what he figures $1 today, if invested at 8.38 percent a year, will be worth in twenty years. He calls the difference "lost investment earnings."

While I have used 6.5 percent, he used 8.38 percent, partly to get the final number to be exactly $5. He also thinks 8.38 percent is on the conservative side, compared with twenty-year market returns of 10 to 12 percent. I felt more comfortable using 6.5 percent for my calculations because there have been long periods when the market has languished; between 1968 and 1978, for example, it lost 45 percent of its value. Historically, the market has returned about 7 percent. And there are plenty of economists who predict weak returns for the next twenty years. But if you're a market bull, that can of soda looks even more expensive.

But what's important here is the concept, not the exact numbers. You can save a lot of money, or cut your expenses dramatically, if you are willing to pay attention to the little things that add up to big money over time.

In another one of his columns, Jeff described what he calls the "Whopper Test" for spending money. For instance, if you pay $40 for a meal, is it ten times better than a Burger King Whopper with cheese? If not, Jeff says, it fails his Whopper Test. What Jeff is getting at is your sense of value. After you spend money for something, do you honestly feel you got good value? For me, most expensive restaurant meals fail this test. And I almost never feel I get value for an expensive hotel or motel room, where I usually just sleep for a few hours. Then again, some people would be aghast at what I spend for bicycles and related equipment.

Some expenditures, of course, pass his Whopper Test more easily than others. Home repairs, for instance, usually pass because you'll probably get some of that money back when you sell your home. A fancy car may or may not pass, depending on your personal situation and how much your ego is linked to what you drive.

You need to be flexible. As Jeff put it in his Whopper Test column: "Over time, of course, one's sense of value evolves, so it pays to readminister the Whopper Test once in a while. As a cost-saving move, I used to change the oil in my cars myself. Then a day came when I decided it really was worth 10 or 15 bucks to avoid climbing under there and getting that stuff in my face." He continued: "In the same way, I've decided it's worth $4 to take my pickup to the car wash. But only in the winter. In the warm months, I scrub it myself."

Where to draw the line on all this is, naturally, up to your individual preferences and tolerances and your sense of value. In most of our lives, however, there's a lot of financial slack that can be taken up with minimal change. The payoff can be early retirement.

These suggestions, of course, only scratch the surface. If you search for "cutting expenses" on an Internet search engine, you'll find hundreds of ideas to consider. A couple of interesting sites are mightybargainhunter.com and bloggingawaydebt.com. The first is operated by John Wedding in King George, Virginia, who works as a physicist in his day job. He loves figuring out ways to save money. "My parents were frugal," he said. "I guess it rubbed off on me." Tricia Sperry in Calumet, Michigan, runs the second. The site allows you to see exactly how she and her husband are cutting expenses and saving money to pay down their credit card debt.

THE PLASTIC TRAP AND OTHER DEBT

Spending too much becomes even more critical if you're doing it on credit. Relax. Even though it's hard to overstate the problem, this is not another lecture on the danger of credit card debt. You know about that already. This is just a reminder that such debt can imperil your retirement plans.

Fred Waddell, the money-management specialist who trains financial counselors, always includes in his seminars a section on eliminating deficits, or "reducing negative cash flow." In simple terms, this means retiring with as little debt as possible—preferably none. "Any kind of debt has to be looked at as a mortgage of future income," Waddell said. "It is a claim against future income. It becomes very difficult to calculate how much you're going to live on in retirement if the amount of money you're using in your calculations is not really yours but belongs to your creditors."

He says as you approach retirement you should reduce your outstanding debt to as close to zero as possible. All debt is not created equal, however. Credit card debt and debt for a depreciating asset, like a car, should be paid off first, starting with the debt that carries the highest interest. Some mortgage debt may be tolerable because the underlying asset, a house, is presumably appreciating in value, effectively reducing the interest costs. "Some advisers say pay off all debt, including mortgage debt," Waddell said. "I would say pay off the mortgage debt if possible. But certainly pay off all other debt like credit cards and car loans. If you're paying fourteen to seventeen percent interest on credit card debt and you pay that off, it's like earning fourteen to seventeen percent on your money."

If there were no early-withdrawal penalties involved, would he advise dipping into retirement savings to pay off such debt? "Yes," was his immediate reply. "And that's a no-brainer now that savings are earning only a few percent and credit cards are charging up to eighteen percent, and sometimes more, on balances." He also advises that as you approach retirement, you consider making prepayments on your mortgage. "I did this and it worked out pretty well," he said. "All my investments were in stocks, so I looked on my mortgage prepayments as the missing bond portion of my portfolio." The result of mortgage prepayments can be dramatic, even if you are close to having your house paid for.

For instance, let's assume that in January 1980 you signed a $250,000 home mortgage with a 7 percent thirty-year fixed-rate loan. That means if you made the regular monthly payments of $1,663.26 for thirty years, or 360 months, your house would be paid for in January 2010. But if in January 2003 you started paying an extra $500 a month on the mortgage, you would pay the loan off one year and eleven months sooner (in February 2008) and save $8,770.66 in interest.

Now let's assume that with this same mortgage, you had decided to start making those $500-a-month prepayments in January 1990. That would have cut seven years and eight months off your loan and your house would have been paid for in May 2002. Interest saved: $78,555.75.

There are several good mortgage calculators on the Web where you can plug in the numbers to make them fit your particular situation. My favorite, and the one I used for these calculations, is on the Bloomberg Web site (www.bloomberg.com). Prepayment is not limited to mortgages, of course. It works with credit card bills too. However you do it, getting rid of debt will certainly make your retirement easier and will probably allow it to happen sooner. Remember, when you reduce debt—or cut other expenses—you increase income.

A Special Invitation (to Anyone)

Like most of us, Ann Hamman—who died in June 2003 at age ninety-five—was deluged with mail offering "preapproved" credit cards and various lines of credit from banks and financial services companies, large and small. Gold cards, platinum cards, titanium cards. Credit lines of as much as $100,000. During the final few years of her life, however, Ann Hamman never saw these offers. That is because she lived in an assisted-living residence in Homestead, Florida. She suffered from memory problems and needed help with daily activities; she was unable to prepare meals or manage a bank account. Her mail went to her son, Henry Hamman, who lived nearby in Miami. Hamman, who had his mother's power of attorney, said he was appalled at the mail solicitations she received. "When you market indiscriminately to the elderly and the susceptible, I think it's pretty reprehensible," he said. "This is the financial equivalent of handing a loaded gun to a kid."

He is particularly angry about a check his mother received from Household Bank in Las Vegas, a subsidiary of Household International. The check was for $1,500.02. All Ann Hamman had to do was endorse it and, presto, the money would be hers—along with a legal obligation to repay the loan in monthly installments of $55.72 for forty-eight months. That means that she would repay $2,674.56, which translates to an annual interest rate of 31.945 percent. "If this check had fallen into her hands, it's entirely conceivable that she might have used it and not really known what she was doing," Hamman said.

A spokeswoman for Household International, which is based in Prospect Heights, Illinois, said her company did not specifically single out older people for such solicitations. She agreed that the 31.945 percent rate offered to Ann Hamman was "stunning."

Henry Hamman was also puzzled that many of the offers cited his mother's excellent credit history as a reason for offering her up to $100,000 of credit. "She didn't have any credit," he said. "She had no assets other than her pension and Social Security and hadn't owned a home since the 1960s. She even got credit offers beyond the grave, including thirty thousand dollars for an automobile loan. Either there was a credit report mix-up or this is the biggest bunch of hooey I've ever seen." A spokeswoman in Washington for the American Bankers Association, a lobbying group, said that members "look at creditworthiness" before making credit card offers.

Ann Hamman grew up in Oklahoma and during World War II was a lieutenant in the Women's Army Corps, serving in Italy and Algeria. She later worked in Indiana as a consumer education agent and as a food editor at the *Evansville Courier*. After retiring, she served in the Peace Corps in Belize for two years. "She was always a very independent person who stood up for folks who couldn't stand up for themselves," her son said. "These credit offers would have upset her because of the damage they can do to people who aren't financially sophisticated." The seemingly personal solicitations can also prove seductive to the psychologically vulnerable. Ann Hamman was lucky that she had her son to look out for her in these matters. Many older people who are on their own—especially if they are homebound, lonely, or confused—can easily fall victim to such practices that, while not illegal, are certainly questionable.

Travis B. Plunkett, the legislative director of the Consumer Federation of America, based in Washington, D.C., said "indiscriminate and reckless marketing" had become the rule in the credit card industry, which mails out billions of solicitations each year. "Their business model, the way they profit, is to make risky loans to people who often don't have the financial skills to know whether it's right or not," he added. "They'll give a credit card to anything that moves."

Consider the case involving the late Doug X. Ping. Doug was a Shar-Pei who was struck by a car and killed in 1994, when he was five. Gordon Krelove, the dog's owner, who had brought the pet to the United States from China, later put Doug's name on some random consumer survey. Soon, Doug received a solicitation from First USA Bank in Wilmington, Delaware, for a National Geographic Society platinum MasterCard with a "solid line of credit" of up to $100,000.

A spokesman for First USA Bank, which is a member of the banking association and a subsidiary of Bank One, said, "We make every effort to ensure that the offers we mail out go to credit-eligible adults."

If you're not a dog, you can take some steps to limit the number of mail solicitations you receive. For a $1 fee, the Web site of the Direct Marketing Association (www.the-dma.org/consumers) allows you to remove your name from its members' mailing lists. There is also an automated toll-free number (1-888-567-8688) that allows you to remove your name from mailing lists provided by the big credit-reporting agencies. But perhaps the best advice on dealing with credit solicitations comes from James A. Guest, the president of Consumers Union, based in Yonkers, New York. "Just throw the stuff in the trash," he said. Better yet, shred it.

LIFE INSURANCE

A lot of people in their fifties are perplexed about life insurance. If they have term insurance, the premiums are probably getting too expensive; if they have universal life that is linked to interest rates, they may be facing higher premiums to maintain coverage. In reality, life insurance is a good place for many people with sufficient assets to cut expenses. They simply may be paying for something they don't really need.

Deena Katz, the financial adviser in Coral Gables, Florida, points out that life insurance "manages risks," adding: "You have it to replace your income or for some specific need for your family when you're not there. If you don't have that need, you don't need the insurance. If you're not providing for your family after your death—say your kids are grown and out on their own—and you're retired with other assets to provide for your spouse, there's no risk to manage."

She advises people in this situation to cancel or cash in their life insurance policies and put the monthly premiums into long-term-care insurance instead. But consult a financial adviser first; if your policy has cash value, you may be able to shelter the proceeds from current taxes.

4

Where Will You Live?

*We were looking for a way to live more simply in jobs that are
more rewarding, that bring value to society and ourselves.*
— KENDRA GOLDEN

Late in 2001, Bill and Donna Taaffe learned that the annual taxes on
their ninety-three-year-old home in Maplewood, New Jersey, a suburb
of New York, would nearly double to $15,800 ($1,317 a month) in the
coming year from $8,200 ($683 a month) because of a reassessment.
In addition, the increase was retroactive to the beginning of 2001,
which meant they owed a lump-sum payment of about $8,000 in ad-
dition to the future monthly increase. The Taaffes fought back and
eventually succeeded in getting the increase lowered to $13,500, or
$1,125 a month. The retroactive payment was reduced to $5,500.
"But it was a huge hit," Bill Taaffe said. "It helped deplete our savings
pretty fast. That increase made things financially very tight for us. It
was almost impossible to make it on our salaries." Bill Taaffe was a
sports editor at the *New York Times* for ten years, and, before that, a
writer for *Sports Illustrated*; Donna Taaffe worked for a nonprofit organization in New Jersey.

By the next summer, the property taxes were increased again and the couple—he was fifty-nine and she was fifty-eight—decided they had had it. "We felt like every dollar we made we were just pouring into the house," Bill Taaffe said. "We were barely keeping our heads above water and had all that stress and anxiety. It just didn't make any sense."

"THE CAT BY THE TAIL"

The Taaffes sold their home in Maplewood, quit their jobs, and moved with their adopted nine-year-old son to Henderson, Nevada, a suburb of Las Vegas, where Donna's cousin—"more like a sister," according to Bill—had moved with her family two years earlier. With the profit from the sale of their house in New Jersey the Taaffes were able to pay cash for a modern home they liked better than their old one and install a swimming pool and Jacuzzi.

Although Bill continues to work—as a freelance writer, mainly of books—he says what he did amounts to a retirement of sorts. "I guess it was a kind of a segue into retirement," he said. "I like doing things on my own terms. That commute into New York was a grind that just got old. But I'm probably never going to fully retire. I'm always going to keep my hand in."

The experience of Bill and Donna Taaffe is worth examining in some detail for two reasons. First, their unorthodox "retirement" is typical of how many baby boomers say they plan to leave their traditional jobs. Second, theirs is a classic example of the importance of where you retire—it is a huge factor in how well you can live and, perhaps, whether you can retire earlier.

Bill estimated that by moving to Nevada, he and his wife cut their expenses by more than half; the property taxes on their new home, for instance, are $2,000 *a year*. And that's in addition to living mortgage-free. While they faced college expenses for their son, Bill said they had already provided for that in their savings.

Comparing Places

Their experience can be quantified by BestPlaces.net and Retire-mentLiving.com, two Web sites mentioned in chapter 2. Since Bill Taaffe commuted into New York City, a comparison of the metro areas was important. According to BestPlaces.net, in 2002 it was 55.2 percent cheaper to live in the Las Vegas area than in New York. In other words, a $44,800 salary in Las Vegas went as far as a $100,000 salary in New York. (Remember, that comparison assumes comparable expenses *and a mortgage payment.*) A home that cost $341,330 in New York was priced at $123,120 in Las Vegas. The overall cost-of-living index, with 100 the national average, was 193.4 in New York and 108 in Las Vegas.

BestPlaces.net allows you to compare smaller cities and towns. Putting Maplewood and Henderson side by side was equally jarring. The median cost of a home in Maplewood in 2002 was $241,120; in Henderson, it was $144,770. Maplewood's property tax rate per $1,000 of assessed valuation was listed at $26.30, compared with $10.20 in Henderson; the national average was $16.43. The Web site also allows you to compare other factors, like people and population, the economy, health, crime, education, climate, and transportation.

These numbers and comparisons, of course, have changed since the Taaffes made their move, which proved to be a model of good timing. That's because home prices have zoomed during the past five years in the fast-growing Las Vegas area. The median price of a house in Henderson, for instance, climbed from $144,700 in 2002 to $482,500 in 2007—not much less than the $484,900 for Maplewood; the 2007 national average was $217,200. The Las Vegas area cost-of-living index rose to 130.8 from 108. The cost-of-living gap narrowed to 33.3 percent from 55.2 percent, meaning it took $66,667 in 2007 instead of $44,800 in 2002 to equal a New York salary of $100,000.

The Taaffes, however, have been heavily shielded from these increases because they don't have a mortgage on their home, for which they paid $184,000 in cash. Someone looking to duplicate their experience would likely have to look somewhere other than

Henderson and Las Vegas. The area has become an example of what happens to communities when they become popular, a phenomenon that will be repeated as the baby boomers retire and move. It also demonstrates another reason to do your homework before you make a retirement decision.

The state of Nevada does have some advantages for retirees that could make somewhere other than the Las Vegas area worth considering. As RetirementLiving.com points out, Nevada is one of seven states with no personal income tax, so there is no tax on retirement income. In addition, homeowners who are at least sixty-two years old and earn $24,016 a year or less are eligible for a rebate of up to $500 or 90 percent of their property taxes. The main reason that taxes are low in Nevada, of course, is casino gambling and the tourists and conventions it attracts. All this money from outsiders generates taxes and other benefits that help keep residents' taxes low. "Henderson overlooks Las Vegas and we can see planes coming in over the valley to land," Bill Taaffe said. "My wife's cousin's husband sometimes says, 'Here comes another planeload of people to pay our taxes.' If you don't gamble, you kind of have the cat by the tail here."

Bill and Donna Taaffe were very deliberate in their decision to move. "We came to the conclusion that we had a choice," Bill Taaffe said. "If I continued working in New York, we would have to move to a smaller house in Maplewood or further out on the train line to a cheaper place with a longer commute. Then in eight years when our son went to college, we would retire and move again. We decided this was crazy. Why not move once, to an area of the country where we knew we could make a go of it? I had a book deal and I knew I could do other books after that. I knew there were all sorts of projects I could do on my own. It was like a zero-sum game. We wanted to move somewhere where if we didn't do anything for the next six years until we were eligible for Social Security, we could still make it. We knew what our house was worth and what we could buy a house for in Nevada."

Their New Jersey house sold in one day—without the services of a real estate agent, so they pocketed the 6 percent commission. They had paid $252,000 for the four-bedroom home in 1996. They sold it for $465,000. After paying off the balance of their mortgage, they walked away with about $250,000. "We were attracted to Nevada because we had been there to visit Donna's cousin in Henderson," Bill said. "We had also lived for two years in Colorado and loved the West. Plus, I knew different parts of the country from work-related travel."

In 2002, they moved to Henderson and lived with Donna's cousin for several weeks until they bought a home. "We found a new home for a fraction of what we were spending in New Jersey, where our house had all sorts of problems and constantly needed fixing," Bill continued. They paid the $184,000 for the Nevada house and put another $30,000 into some additions they wanted, including the pool and Jacuzzi. "In retrospect, the decision was a no-brainer. By moving out here, we have been able to live more comfortably and work at our own pace. Plus, we're living in a place and a home we really like. Our new house has four bedrooms, three baths, and is all on one level, a feature we find very comfortable. Everything out here is less expensive. Prescriptions, restaurants, entertainment, car repairs—you name it. If you don't gamble, you can really make out at the casinos where they have good food at incredible prices. Also, despite being one of the fastest-growing areas in the country, the traffic hassle here is about twenty-five percent of what it was in the New York area. Another really important thing for us has been property taxes, which were $1,500 a year when we moved here and have increased to only $2,000; if we had stayed in our New Jersey house, our taxes would have been more than $20,000 a year by now. But owning our home free and clear—no mortgage payment—that has made the big difference."

The Taaffes' Health Insurance

One wrinkle in the Taaffes' move was health insurance. Bill would have had to work for three more years to formally retire from the

New York Times and have retirement health benefits. "We just didn't want to struggle for three more years," he said. "In addition, we thought it would be much easier for our son to move at nine than at twelve or thirteen. And it's worked out okay for him; he likes it out here." So he continued his company health insurance under a federal plan called COBRA (short for Consolidated Omnibus Budget Reconciliation Act of 1985) that allows participants who leave a job to extend—at their own expense—their health insurance benefits for eighteen months. The price can be hefty. For the Taaffes, it was about $1,000 a month.

"But we took that expense into account," Bill said. "We knew when the eighteen months were up, we would have to go to the open market and buy a family health plan, which is what we did. We took it in stride." (Chapter 6 looks at some health insurance options for people in the same situation as the Taaffes.)

The Taaffes were lucky in that they had relatives in Henderson and knew the area somewhat from previous visits. It can be difficult to pull up roots, leave an area you know and where you have friends and perhaps family, and move to somewhere new. "We were a little worried about Nevada and Las Vegas because of their reputation for being a transient community," Bill said. "That was, and still is to some extent, a negative in my mind. But we haven't really felt a lack of community here. Henderson is family-oriented and the schools are good. It's really not part of the glitz of Las Vegas."

DECISIONS, DECISIONS

Although surveys indicate that a lot of people want to stay put when they retire, those annual "Best Places" articles in personal finance magazines are always a big hit.

I expect there is something of a disconnect between people's responses to these surveys and reality. As mentioned in chapter 2, I wonder if the answers to these survey questions would be different if they explained that staying put may mean you can't retire as early as you might like.

I don't mean to play down the importance of family, friends, community, or one's sense of place. But retiring to a cheaper area doesn't necessarily mean giving up all these things. We live in such a mobile society that most of us have friends and relatives spread across the country. Many of us are living where we are—and maintaining our expensive lifestyles—because of our jobs, not because of family or friends or other ties. The Taaffes, for instance, actually moved closer to some family members when they moved to the Las Vegas area.

Richard E. Mayer, an independent financial consultant in Mineola, New York, agrees. "The baby boomers and their families are spread out all over the place, so retiring to be near family or friends is less of an issue," he said.

If your goal is to retire early, where you decide to live is an extremely important and difficult decision. You do not want to wind up in a place where you are not happy and then quickly make another move.

It's important to do research at Web sites like BestPlaces.net and RetirementLiving.com. It's even more important to vacation in places where you think you might want to retire—and not just at the best times of the year. Go to Arizona or Florida in the summer. Check Maine or Colorado in the winter. Talk to residents and look carefully at the local newspaper. Better yet, if you have the time and money, rent an apartment and live in your chosen town for a few months to really get a feel for the place.

In the early 1990s, Joyce Ensminger and her late husband, Joseph Ensminger, moved from their home state of Kansas to Green Valley, Arizona, a retirement community about twenty miles south of Tucson. They went there because Joseph Ensminger, eighty-two at the time, had been hospitalized with pneumonia, and they were seeking a warmer and drier climate.

In 1999 they moved back.

"Green Valley is a lovely place, but I missed my children and family," said Joyce Ensminger, who was sixty-eight when the couple moved to Arizona. "After all, family is everything." She conceded that she wanted to return more than her husband and that he went along to please her. "Joe had recently had a serious operation, and he felt a little mortal," she said. "He wanted to know that I was all settled before something happened to him."

The Ensmingers were not alone. Many retirees move to another part of the country, then decide to return to where they had lived and worked most of their lives. Usually they long to be closer to family members, often because of failing health or the death of a spouse. Sometimes, they fail to make new friends or otherwise decide that they don't like their new environment as much as they thought. Arizona or Florida can be wonderful in February; August is another story.

Precise figures are difficult to come by, but Charles F. Longino Jr., a gerontologist at Wake Forest University in Winston-Salem, North Carolina, uses census data to estimate that about 5 percent of retirees actually move to another state. Of that share, as many as 10 percent or more may eventually return. According to the most recent available data, eighty-two thousand people over sixty years old moved from New York to Florida between 1985 and 1990, while thirteen thousand moved from Florida to New York.

For the Ensmingers and others like them, the trade-offs were not worth it. Joseph Ensminger was a retired sports referee and sales manager for a safety-glass maker. Joyce Ensminger is a retired public school administrative assistant. They had both been married before and between them had six children, fifteen grandchildren, and three great-grandchildren. They sold their Arizona home and built a new house in Olathe, Kansas, a suburb of Kansas City.

For Joseph Ensminger, his wife's considerations outweighed the Sun Belt's virtues. "However, in many ways Arizona was ideal for me—you wake up every morning and the sun is shining," he said shortly after the move back to Kansas. "But we were twelve hundred miles from Kansas City. One family member had been out once and another twice. To see our family we had to travel there. Now we're back with people we know." He died in 2003, at age ninety-two.

Many retirees who are tempted to leave their new locales, however, decide to remain. A second move can be stressful—and expensive. If you live in an area that has been overdeveloped, you may have trouble selling your home. It took the Ensmingers, for example, several months to sell their Green Valley house; meanwhile, their money was tied up. There are also real estate commissions, moving expenses, and a myriad of incidental costs. That second move can wind up costing tens of thousands of dollars.

In the mid-1990s, Jean S. Beals, then in her seventies, moved to Naples, Florida, from Mount Holly, New Jersey. A retired bank teller, she has been a widow since 1981. Once, during a trip back to New Jersey, she considered returning. "I got homesick," she said. "I thought maybe I shouldn't have moved. I missed my friends and my church." But Beals had something to draw her back to Florida that many retirees there lack: a daughter in Naples and a son in Sarasota. "So I finally decided no," she said. "I have a lovely place in Florida, and I don't like cold weather anymore. Plus my children are near me. It's too stressful for me to move now."

Trendy Has Its Price

I'm always a bit leery of those "Best Places" lists that appear in magazines. For one thing, the lists are usually different each year in *the same magazine.* How can a town be number one or two one year and not even on the list the next? This suggests a certain manufactured ranking. Second, as soon as a town shows up on one of these lists, you can be certain property values will soon start to rise. Many of the features that made the town attractive will melt away as popularity pushes up its population and degrades its services and attractive features. Santa Fe, New Mexico, is a good example of this. Always popular with tourists, the city has become a trendy retirement destination over the last couple of decades and homes have soared in value. A lot of people from Southern California, their bank accounts fat from selling homes whose value skyrocketed in the 1980s and 1990s, moved to Santa Fe and bid up property prices. Throw in a few Hollywood celebrities who buy second homes and the mix has produced a lot of overpriced property. And—although modest by the standards of Los Angeles and New York—traffic and related congestion have taken their toll on the city's quality of life.

One solution is to use those magazine articles as a guide to an area rather than a specific town or city. If you like Santa Fe, for instance, but find it a bit rich for your budget, look sixty-five miles east at Las Vegas, New Mexico. If you use the comparisons provided by BestPlaces.net, you'll find that the climate and terrain are similar; the comfort index for both is in the high seventies, compared with the national average of 44. However, the air quality in Las Vegas is twice as good as that in Santa Fe, and the population of Las Vegas is only about a quarter of Santa Fe's 67,500.

As might be expected from its popularity as a retirement haven, the median age of Santa Fe residents is 41.7, while in Las Vegas it's 35. Perhaps the most telling statistic BestPlaces.net offers about the relative trendiness (and cost of living) of the two cities is that Santa Fe has several Starbucks coffee shops; Las Vegas has none. But trendy has its price. The difference in home prices is striking. The average home cost in the United States is $217,200. In Las Vegas, New Mexico, it is $135,300, while in Santa Fe it is $307,900. The overall cost-of-living index—with the national average at 100—is 87.4 in Las Vegas and 115.4 in Santa Fe. This means it costs about 30 percent more to live in Santa Fe than Las Vegas.

However, as is often the case, the flip side of an area with a lower cost of living is lower incomes. This is the case in Las Vegas, where average per capita income is $15,951 a year and average annual household income is $29,368; the same figures for Santa Fe are $29,390 and $46,429, respectively. The national averages are $24,020 and $44,684. As might be expected, the unemployment rate in Las Vegas is 7.3 percent, compared with 4.7 percent in Santa Fe, which has a lot of tourism-related jobs. Also, certain categories of crime are higher in Las Vegas than in Santa Fe or the national average.

Las Vegas certainly does not have the amenities and shopping of Santa Fe. However, it takes less than an hour to drive to Santa Fe on Interstate 25. So traveling there for dinner or to attend a cultural event is relatively easy.

While there are many reasons why New Mexico is an attractive state, Tom Wetzel of RetirementLiving.com points out that the state's tax laws can be particularly tough on the retired. New Mexico is one of seven states he cites that have relatively high top-tax brackets and fully tax most retirement income. The other six are Connecticut, Minnesota, Nebraska, Rhode Island, Vermont, and Wisconsin.

These comparisons are easy to do on your own. All you need is a good map and Internet access. Let's look at one more example, this time in Florida.

Naples, with a population of 22,000 on the Gulf Coast of south Florida, is often mentioned as a top retirement spot. Like Santa Fe, it's very nice. Also like Santa Fe, it's pricey.

However, about seventy-five miles to the north is Port Charlotte, with a population of about 50,000. Port Charlotte's big advantage over Naples is lower home prices. The median price of a house there is $240,100, compared with $873,500 in Naples and the nationwide average of $217,200. The cost-of-living index for Port Charlotte is 87; for Naples, it's 251. Remember, the national average is 100.

Not surprisingly, the median age in Port Charlotte, 47.8, is considerably lower than the 61.5 in Naples. The average per capita income in Port Charlotte is $20,091, below the national average of $24,020. For Naples, it's $62,891. Household income in Port Charlotte is $37,646, compared with $73,667 in Naples and $44,684 nationally.

If you like Florida but can't afford Naples, Port Charlotte is clearly a reasonable alternative. It's close enough to Naples for an easy visit.

A plus no matter where you live in Florida: like Nevada, it is one of the seven states with no personal income tax.

Auto Expenses

For more evidence of the wide variations in costs of living around the country, consider a 2006 study by Runzheimer International (www.runzheimer.com), a big management consulting firm, on automobile insurance expenses.

Runzheimer looked at the annual costs of insurance coverage for a new midsize sedan driven within a fifty-mile radius of a city. It used rates for both male and female drivers with clean driving records; the coverage included comprehensive, collision, bodily injury, property damage, and uninsured motorist coverage. The range was staggering, from almost $6,000 in Detroit, Michigan, to less than $1,000 in Roanoke, Virginia.

Here are the five most expensive cities:

Detroit	$5,894
Philadelphia	$4,440
Newark, New Jersey	$3,977
New York City	$3,430
Los Angeles	$3,303

The five least expensive cities were:

Roanoke, Virginia	$912
Chattanooga, Tennessee	$980
Nashville, Tennessee	$1,040
Green Bay, Wisconsin	$1,042
Raleigh, North Carolina	$1,057

Runzheimer officials have cited fewer accidents, vehicle thefts, and collision damage repair bills in places like Roanoke as reasons for lower premiums.

Another study by the firm found that it costs almost twice as much to maintain a car in San Francisco as it does in Bismarck, North Dakota. The per-mile costs were based on a typical midsize vehicle driven fifteen thousand miles a year and retained for four years. Maintenance expenses included normal and preventive procedures like oil changes, lubrication, and brake and exhaust system inspections: the stuff you're supposed to do according to your car's service manual. They do not include fuel, insurance, tires, or the costs of the car itself.

The most expensive cities, along with the per-mile maintenance costs for each:

San Francisco	6.79 cents
New York City	6.38 cents
Hempstead (Long Island)	5.62 cents
Honolulu	5.49 cents
Chicago	5.21 cents
Miami	5.17 cents
Newark, New Jersey	5.13 cents
St. Louis	5.13 cents
Stamford, Connecticut	5.09 cents
Sacramento, California	5.01 cents
Seattle	5.01 cents

The least expensive cities:

Bismarck, North Dakota	3.56 cents
Casper, Wyoming	3.64 cents
Richmond, Virginia	3.68 cents
Lubbock, Texas	3.76 cents
Billings, Montana	3.80 cents
Omaha, Nebraska	3.80 cents
Henderson, Kentucky	3.88 cents
Jackson, Mississippi	3.88 cents
Burlington, Vermont	3.92 cents
Evansville, Indiana	3.92 cents
Montgomery, Alabama	3.92 cents
Portland, Maine	3.92 cents

While this may seem like small change, that 1.09-cent difference between Portland, Maine, and Seattle adds up to $163.50 if you drive a car fifteen thousand miles.

Dream Towns

Despite my concern about "Best Places" articles in magazines, there are a couple I would like to mention because of their links to baby boomers. Both appeared in *AARP The Magazine*, which has made a lot of editorial changes in recent years to court boomers as they approach retirement.

One appeared in the July–August 2006 issue of the magazine and promoted five cities that offer "culture, cachet, or, in some cases, just peace and quiet." The article added that for each one, "it doesn't cost a fortune to live there." The five are:

Las Cruces, New Mexico
Charleston, South Carolina
Rehoboth Beach, Delaware
Memphis, Tennessee
St. George, Utah

The version of the article online includes a link to a "Location Scout" that allows you to rate the importance of different features—from home prices to tax levels to cultural attractions. You can then pull out the map to find nearby towns with even lower expenses.

The other article was in the magazine's May–June 2003 issue and is particularly significant because it captures the choices boomers make themselves. AARP asked boomers for their "dream town" and listed the top fifteen responses. The magazine says the list shows this generation once again breaking the rules by rejecting traditional retirement communities and opting for places with appealing cultural and recreational lifestyles. According to the survey, boomers seek places with a "youthful vibe," great medical facilities, and sophisticated restaurants. As pointed out in chapter 2, many boomers will continue working, but on their own terms. This is reinforced by the magazine's survey, which says the boomers will first pick a place they like and then look for a job or become an entrepreneur, rather than follow a job to a place.

Here are the boomers' choices, according to *AARP The Magazine*:

1. Loveland/Fort Collins, Colorado
2. Bellingham, Washington
3. Raleigh/Durham/Chapel Hill, North Carolina
4. Sarasota, Florida
5. Fayetteville, Arkansas
6. Charleston, South Carolina
7. Asheville, North Carolina
8. San Diego, California
9. San Antonio, Texas
10. Santa Fe, New Mexico
11. Gainesville, Florida
12. Iowa City, Iowa
13. Portsmouth, New Hampshire
14. Spokane, Washington
15. Ashland, Oregon

By the way, the headline on the press release announcing the survey was surely written by a boomer: "*AARP The Magazine* Names the 15 Best Places to Reinvent Your Life."

State and Local Taxes

Information from sites like BestPlaces.net and RetirementLiving .com can give you a pretty good idea of state taxes around the country. But the wild card is property taxes, which are mainly locally imposed and can vary widely within a state and even within a county. To get precise information, you will have to check the local tax rate for the town you're considering. You'll also need to check the assessment standards—that is, what percentage of a property's assessed valuation is taxed. This can be very important. One locality, for instance, may have a high rate but tax only a small percentage of assessed valuation; conversely, another locality may have a low rate but tax more of a home's assessed value, which could result in higher taxes than the first case.

The Tax Foundation, a nonprofit research organization in Washington, D.C., has a Web site (www.taxfoundation.org) that can help. Among other things, it lists the per capita property taxes in the fifty states and the District of Columbia. Use the numbers with caution; they are only a rough guide because of the wide local variations in property taxes. Also, these are *per capita* figures, which include the entire population of a state, not just property owners; individual property taxes are much higher than the per capita amount. It is the *ranking* that can be a helpful guide.

Here's the Tax Foundation's most recent list, ranked from highest to lowest according to the per capita amount:

New Jersey ($2,099)
Connecticut ($1,944)
New Hampshire ($1,940)
District of Columbia ($1,856)
New York ($1,677)
Rhode Island ($1,629)
Maine ($1,596)
Massachusetts ($1,532)
Vermont ($1,531)
Illinois ($1,407)
Wyoming ($1,352)
Wisconsin ($1,350)
Alaska ($1,306)
Texas ($1,254)
Kansas ($1,187)
Michigan ($1,186)
Nebraska ($1,148)

Maryland ($1,082)
Iowa ($1,080)
Florida ($1,064)
Montana ($1,034)
Virginia ($1,031)
Washington ($1,029)
Colorado ($1,026)
Pennsylvania ($1,010)
Ohio ($981)
Indiana ($975)
Minnesota ($965)
Oregon ($963)
California ($963)
Nevada ($920)
North Dakota ($919)
South Dakota ($915)
South Carolina ($882)
Georgia ($880)
Arizona ($848)
Idaho ($777)
Missouri ($747)
North Carolina ($713)
Utah ($689)
Mississippi ($641)
Tennessee ($608)
Hawaii ($571)
Delaware ($546)
West Virginia ($540)
Kentucky ($516)
Louisiana ($502)
Oklahoma ($465)
New Mexico ($441)
Arkansas ($400)
Alabama ($367)

RetirementLiving.com's Tom Wetzel says that because of the incredible variations in property taxes, it is extremely difficult to come to a definitive conclusion about which state is the least expensive. However, his Web site contains a ranking of states according to the total tax burden—expressed as a percentage of income—that each state imposes on its residents. The data come from the Census Bureau and include local property taxes, sales taxes, income taxes, and so on. They do not include any federal taxes, but they do take into account local and state taxes on businesses.

According to this list, the five states with the highest state and local tax burdens are Vermont, Maine, New York, Rhode Island, and Ohio (tied with Hawaii). The five lowest are Alaska, New Hampshire, Tennessee, Delaware, and Alabama. If the District of Columbia were ranked with the states, it would stand at number five—with its residents paying 12.5 percent of their income for local taxes. The United States average is 11.06 percent. Here's the complete list of states, with the tax burden for each shown as a percentage of income.

Vermont (14.1 percent)
Maine (14.0 percent)
New York (13.8 percent)
Rhode Island (12.7 percent)
Ohio (12.4 percent)
Hawaii (12.4 percent)
Wisconsin (12.3 percent)
Connecticut (12.2 percent)
Nebraska (11.9 percent)
New Jersey (11.6 percent)
Minnesota (11.5 percent)
California (11.5 percent)
Michigan (11.2 percent)
Kansas (11.2 percent)
Washington (11.1 percent)
Louisiana (11.0 percent)

Iowa (11.0 percent)
North Carolina (11.0 percent)
Kentucky (10.9 percent)
West Virginia (10.9 percent)
Illinois (10.8 percent)
Maryland (10.8 percent)
Pennsylvania (10.8 percent)
Indiana (10.7 percent)
South Carolina (10.7 percent)
Utah (10.7 percent)
Massachusetts (10.6 percent)
Mississippi (10.5 percent)
Colorado (10.4 percent)
Arizona (10.3 percent)
Arkansas (10.3 percent)
Georgia (10.3 percent)
Virginia (10.2 percent)
Missouri (10.1 percent)
Idaho (10.1 percent)
Nevada (10.1 percent)
Oregon (10.0 percent)
Florida (10.0 percent)
North Dakota (9.9 percent)
New Mexico (9.8 percent)
Montana (9.7 percent)
Wyoming (9.5 percent)
Texas (9.3 percent)
South Dakota (9.0 percent)
Oklahoma (9.0 percent)
Alabama (8.8 percent)
Delaware (8.8 percent)
Tennessee (8.5 percent)
New Hampshire (8.0 percent)
Alaska (6.6 percent)

Though neither the per capita ranking nor the income-linked ranking is perfect, the second list is probably more valuable for the average person than the per capita list because of distortions from widely varying populations and incomes among the states. "This is the most realistic tax-burden charge I could find," Wetzel said. He pointed out that many traditionally low-tax states do not have the same level of services and education as do many higher-tax states. "But there are some very nice areas in these states," he said. "And if you don't have kids, the quality of schools may not be a factor. If you're just looking for a residence with not a lot of service—and you're not looking for a great appreciation on your property— then one of these states might be the place for you."

Another collection of tax data on Wetzel's site that can be helpful is a summary from a study by the National Association of Home Builders that analyzes and compares property tax revenue for 2005 in the various states. It's contained in the June 2007 issue of *Retirement Living News*, Wetzel's newsletter that is archived on his site.

RetirementLiving.com also provides roundups of the tax situation in each state. For instance, five states—Alaska, Delaware, Montana, New Hampshire, and Oregon—have no sales tax. Seven states have no personal income tax: Alaska, Florida, Nevada, South Dakota, Texas, Washington, and Wyoming. New Hampshire and Tennessee collect income tax only on dividend and interest income.

Of the states that do have income taxes, twenty-six do not tax Social Security benefits. Some states have limited exemptions for different kinds of pensions.

Wetzel warns that sales taxes should be considered closely. Oklahoma, for instance, has a state sales tax of only 4.5 percent. But city and county governments can increase that by up to 4.25 percentage points, which means the total sales tax could be as high as 8.75 percent, depending on where you live in the state. The same is true in Louisiana, where a state rate of 4 percent can reach 10.75 percent locally. "People need to look at the total tax picture as they try to shelter themselves as much as possible," Wetzel said. "Retirees may discover that some states are not the tax havens they are reported to be. A state may look inexpensive because it has no income tax, but it may have high property taxes or sales taxes. So the presence or absence of a state income tax may not be the best criterion for selecting a retirement destination. You also need to consider what tax relief is available for seniors."

While his site doesn't give specific information on local property taxes because they are so variable, it does give information on different statewide property tax breaks available to retirees. Wetzel stresses, however, that taxes and living costs are not the only factors you should consider in looking for a place to live. He cited ten considerations that he thought were important when surveying a town or area, but emphasized that the order of the list should be shuffled according to individual needs and tastes. Or an item can be eliminated if it doesn't concern you. Here's his top ten list:

1. cost of living (including taxes)
2. climate
3. medical care
4. culture
5. distance from family and friends
6. crime
7. recreational opportunities
8. part-time employment opportunities
9. nearest airport
10. quality of restaurants

"A lot of people say they want to continue to work, at least part-time, in retirement, so they need to consider work opportunities," he said. "In a lot of rural areas, there are no Medicare HMO operations, and some physicians aren't taking new Medicare patients because the fees are being cut; perhaps you have a health problem that requires you to be near a good medical center. A retired music professor might move cultural opportunities higher on the list. Maybe you like to eat out a lot, or maybe you don't care about restaurants.

How important is climate? All these things, not just taxes and living costs, need to be taken into consideration."

Don't Take My Word for It

When looking at comparative data on home prices around the country, be sure you understand the difference between average and median prices. You'll see both used, and they can provide sharply different pictures of the same situation. The average home price is the total value of a given number of homes divided by the number of homes. The median is the midpoint in a range of home prices: half fall above it, half fall below. It's good to look at the median, because the average can be skewed high by a few expensive homes. Of course, what you can't tell from the median alone is how far above and below the middle the range extends.

Bert Sperling of BestPlaces.net says a rule of thumb he follows is that the median price of homes is usually about 30 percent less than the average. Also keep in mind that data are going to vary—sometimes widely—depending on their sources. The best way to find out about home prices in an area in which you are interested is to go there and get a firsthand look and talk to local real estate agents.

It's also a good idea to take a short-term subscription to the local newspaper so you can study its real estate section. Most papers will sell three-month or six-month mail subscriptions. Many have Web sites providing access to much of their classified advertising, including real estate. It's still a good idea to get the printed paper because of photographs and display ads that may not be on a Web site. Also, getting the actual paper can help give you a better feeling for the community.

You can check out homes at www.Realtor.com, a Web site that allows you to search for a home by type (number of bedrooms and baths, for example) and price in cities and towns all over the country. Many of the listings have pictures and some have "virtual tours" that allow you to see panoramic views of various sections of a house, sometimes including a glimpse of its neighborhood. Another helpful site is Zillow.com, which allows you to find the estimated "going price" of a home.

Whenever I travel around the country I collect the little "real estate for sale" booklets you often see in roadside restaurants, malls, and real estate offices. Whether I look at home prices on the Internet, in newspapers, or in these booklets, I am constantly astounded at how low the prices are once you get out of the major metropolitan areas, particularly on the East Coast and West Coast. You can find an acceptable house for a lot less money. Period. Or, if you want to buy a house equal in value to the one you're moving from in a high-price area, you'll get a lot more for your money. A $400,000 home in Arkansas is going to be spectacular compared with a $400,000 house in San Francisco or New York.

I recently took a car trip through the eastern part of West Virginia just south of Hagerstown, Maryland, and on through the Blue Ridge Mountains of Virginia. It's a beautiful area of the country. As usual, I picked up several real estate booklets along the way. While there were certainly plenty of homes listed in the $200,000 to $300,000 price range, consider the following:

- A new home on a one-acre wooded lot. It has three bedrooms, two baths, vaulted ceilings, fully equipped kitchen, a fireplace, basement, and a deck with a hot tub. Asking price: $149,900.
- A two-story log home on five acres. It has three bedrooms and two baths. Price: $95,000.
- A ranch house on 1.77 acres. It has three bedrooms, two baths, a fireplace, deck, and a double garage. Price $119,000.

Of course, by the time this book is published, these houses will have been long sold and comparable houses may have risen in price. These houses may not match your personal taste or be in an area in which you wish to live. But you get the idea.

By the way, if you're living in a cramped New York apartment that costs $300,000 a bedroom or in a $1 million four-room bungalow in California, there was a house for sale in West Virginia the likes of which might command your attention. It is a four-story brick and stone colonial with 7,000 square feet of space. Situated on 3.5 landscaped acres, it has six bedrooms, five full baths, and two half baths. It also has a finished basement and porches on two levels. The price: $580,000.

DRIVING DOWN STRESS

Jim and Kendra Golden made looking for a place to live a way of life, at least for a while. In the spring of 1999, the Goldens, both fifty-two at the time, left their jobs in New Jersey—he was an electrical engineer, she a lawyer—and took to the open road in a thirty-two-foot motor home. They had sold their house in Bergen County and were seeking a new place to live and a new life. They were looking for less stress and for new careers with rewards beyond money. Their son and daughter were both grown and on their own. "We were looking for a way to live more simply in jobs that are more rewarding, that bring value to society and ourselves," Kendra said the following year in an interview for my "Seniority" column in the *New York Times*. "Our former jobs were mentally challenging, but we didn't always have a good sense when we went to bed at night that we were doing good for humanity or having a good life. For example, my job as a partner in a law firm involved a lot of foreclosure work. That was very stressful. Nobody's ever happy to see you coming."

Jim said he cherished the freedom of their nomadic life. "What has appealed to me has been not putting an automatic time limit on our travel, to just travel until it feels right to settle down," he said. "This has been a refreshing experience. My back and neck used to hurt from stress, but not any more." The Goldens even considered continuing their mobile life indefinitely, like the Hofmeisters in chapter 3.

After eighteen months of crisscrossing America—especially the West, to which they were particularly attracted—the Goldens settled in a small town on the Olympic Peninsula in Washington, northwest of Seattle. "The primary reason we stopped traveling was that we wanted to be part of a community again," Kendra said. They bought a house that cost less than half the price they had gotten for their former home in New Jersey. The new house, however, is much smaller. "This area is attracting a lot of people from California, so it's not the housing bargain that some parts of the country are," Jim said.

Although they were both raised in urban environments—he in the Atlanta area, she near Chicago—the two have adjusted well to small-town life. "We wanted off the fast track," Jim said. They especially like the scenic beauty of the area. They still have the motor home and use it for vacations, including a recent three-week trip through the Southwest.

Both are working, but in different careers. In New Jersey, Jim worked mainly in the sales and management areas of electrical engineering. He now works as a computer consultant for a nonprofit concern that provides long-term employment for people with disabilities. Kendra, who says she has no plans to ever again practice law, works for a nonprofit center for arts and education.

"Our life has radically changed," Jim said. "We make substantially less money. But we have a very rich life without a lot of money. Back east, the automatic thing was to go out to an expensive place for dinner. Here, we are less likely to do that. We might go to someone's house for a meal, or just take a hike together."

"We are very happy," Kendra added. "We love being in a small town as opposed to a suburban metropolitan area."

Her husband added: "Never say never, but I don't ever see us coming back to a big urban community. I'm busier than I've ever been before. Sometimes I miss the freedom of our life on the road. But we know we can always go back on the road again if our life doesn't have the same appeal in a few years."

Kendra agreed. "I can see us hitting the road again in the motor home more than I can see us returning to our previous lives," she said.

5

Key No. 1: Your House

I have no children. I want to spend my last dime with my last breath.
— ALECK TOWNSLEY

For most people, the most important asset is the equity in their homes. This is especially true for those who have owned a house for fifteen years or more in a high-cost urban area. Even taking into account the 2007 slump in the housing market (which I'll discuss later in this chapter), the appreciation in real estate prices in these sections of the country has been staggering. These homeowners are sitting on assets that could unlock the door to early retirement. Their homes are like piggy banks containing the money they "deposited" over the years as they paid their mortgages and their property appreciated in value.

Take the case of Ron Martin.

Martin, a finishing contractor in San Diego, California, plans to "retire" to Durango, Colorado, when his youngest son graduates from high school in the spring of 2008.

In 2005, he paid a little more than $300,000 for a Durango town house, which he is renting until he moves there. He believes it is now worth about $400,000. Six months after he bought the Durango home, he sold his home in San Diego—making enough money to cover the cost of the new house.

"The San Diego housing market peaked in the summer of 2005," Martin said. "I sold to take advantage of that." He currently lives in a rental house in San Diego. "My dream was not to own a trophy home in Durango," he added. "What would I do? Be older and sit around in my trophy home? I want to ski and mountain bike. I want to run the rivers."

Not surprisingly, he bristles at the term *retire*.

"*Retire* is not the right word," said Martin, who will be fifty-one when he makes the move. "It's a lifestyle shift. I might continue doing what I'm doing now. Or I might buy an old Victorian house, restore it, sell it, and buy another. I want to work at my own pace. I want to get out of the rat race where you have to keep the money machine running all the time."

Martin lived in Colorado as a child; that's one of the things that attracted him to Durango, an upscale town of about 14,000 in the southwestern mountains of the state. Another was Fort Lewis College. "I like the fact that there's a four-year college there," he said. "It brings a lot of things to town. A town that small would be very incomplete if it didn't have something like a college." He added: "I hope everybody in the world doesn't try to move there. It's not for everybody."

Martin's decision fits a pattern described by Blanche Evans, the editor of RealtyTimes.com, an online real estate news service based in Dallas, Texas. "Many boomers are empty-nesters," she said. "There is a tremendous move toward condos and smaller, low-maintenance homes. The boomers want to pursue their own interests. They don't want to spend time on home maintenance. They don't want a trophy house. Many have done that already."

MORE THAN A PLACE TO LIVE

The Office of Federal Housing Enterprise Oversight (OFHEO), a government agency that tracks changes in home values, has a Web site (www.ofheo.gov) with all kinds of data on home prices around the United States. For instance, average home values across the United States increased 309.8 percent from 1980 through the first quarter of 2007. Between 2002 and 2007, the gain was 53.5 percent. Housing prices even recorded a 4.3 percent increase between the first quarter of 2006 and the first quarter of 2007—not astronomical but pretty good in what was called a bad housing market.

For those living in New England, the Pacific Coast area, or the Middle Atlantic states, the average increases were much higher. For New England, the gain since 1980 was 529.7 percent, with the five-year period and the most recent year coming in at 50.6 percent and 1.1 percent, respectively. For the Pacific Coast, it was 499.4 percent, 89.1 percent, and 4.0 percent. For the Middle Atlantic states, it was 439.4 percent, 63.8 percent, and 4.2 percent.

Remember that these gains are averages. There are some areas within these regions that had much bigger gains, some much smaller. The difference in home values, as well as price gains, within a relatively small area can be dramatic. For instance, in 2003 the *Wall Street Journal* listed median values (half are above, half are below) for homes in three neighborhoods of Scottsdale, Arizona, an upscale part of the sprawling Phoenix metropolitan area, of $405,000, $496,000, and $428,000. Yet for that same year BestPlaces.net put the median value of Scottsdale homes at $195,620. Why the big difference? Well, there are twenty zip codes in Scottsdale, and the newspaper had selected the median values of homes in three of the most expensive, 85259, 85255, and 85262. BestPlaces.net's figure took all the zip codes into account. These same kinds of gaps can also occur for percentage increases in home values depending on the locations within a specific town. For 2007, BestPlaces.net put the median value of homes in Scottsdale at $552,500.

Housing Across the United States

OFHEO used nine regional divisions created by the U.S. Census Bureau (see figure 3).

Figure 4 shows the agency's ranking of the nine regions. I have

Figure 3

U.S. Census Divisions

ranked them according to changes since 1980, which are the most meaningful figures for most baby boomers. The relatively small increases for the quarter and the year reflect the housing slump that started in 2006 and hit hardest in areas that had posted the fastest growth during the previous few years.

The agency's Web site offers a lot more information on home prices, including a state-by-state ranking for various time periods as well as a ranking of 285 metropolitan statistical areas, or MSAs, each of which can involve more than one state.

Here's a list of the states and the District of Columbia with the annual percentage increase in home prices for the year and five years ended March 31, 2007, as well as the period from 1980 to March 31, 2007. Again, I have ranked the states according to their total gains since 1980.

Figure 4

Changes in House Prices Around the Country

In recent years, real estate has risen in value much more rapidly, on average, in some regions of the country than in others. The regions in the chart are the Census Bureau divisions shown in figure 3. The data is for time periods ended September 30, 2002.

Region	Change in the most recent...			Change since 1980	Rank
	Quarter	Year	Five years		
New England	+0.03%	+1.1%	+50.6%	+529.7%	1
Pacific	+0.06	+4.0	+89.9	+499.4	2
Middle Atlantic	+0.5	+4.2	+63.8	+439.4	3
South Atlantic	+0.5	+5.1	+66.2	+329.8	4
National average	+0.5	+4.3	+53.5	+309.8	
Mountain	+1.1	+7.5	+58.6	+287.1	5
East North Central	+0.3	+2.3	+24.7	+222.3	6
West North Central	+0.7	+3.5	+31.8	+205.4	7
East South Central	+1.0	+6.6	+30.2	+189.4	8
West South Central	+1.1	+6.8	+29.8	+126.9	9

Source: Office of Federal Housing Enterprise Oversight

State	1-Year	5-Year	Since 1980
Massachusetts	−0.56	43.72	626.29
New York	3.03	63.89	566.23
Washington, D.C.	5.91	106.97	562.03
California	1.19	98.8	541.25
Rhode Island	1.50	75.91	512.49
New Jersey	3.82	74.06	485.18
Hawaii	4.43	108.89	446.52
Maryland	6.37	96.09	440.14
Maine	3.22	55.94	420.90
Delaware	5.21	67.94	408.30
New Hampshire	1.07	49.17	406.42
Washington	11.63	67.17	398.38
Florida	4.34	102.12	391.76
Connecticut	3.26	56.19	385.11
Virginia	5.42	78.53	374.16
Oregon	10.77	69.00	361.52
Vermont	7.12	63.67	359.43

Arizona	5.22	93.76	332.35
Pennsylvania	5.54	54.21	312.16
Nevada	0.60	95.75	311.68
National average	**4.25**	**53.53**	**309.75**
Illinois	4.87	41.31	283.64
Montana	11.68	62.17	282.77
Minnesota	2.53	40.25	276.42
Utah	17.01	48.29	269.99
Colorado	3.30	21.15	269.91
Idaho	12.27	64.25	253.03
Georgia	5.02	27.95	242.55
North Carolina	7.99	32.16	237.23
New Mexico	11.21	57.12	235.57
Wisconsin	3.49	34.57	234.14
South Carolina	7.59	35.50	222.63
Michigan	−0.66	14.26	220.85
Tennessee	7.06	30.85	204.91
Missouri	3.97	31.56	204.67
Kentucky	4.39	25.09	190.10
South Dakota	6.36	32.57	187.77
Alabama	6.96	33.21	184.19
Alaska	7.02	53.69	178.74
Ohio	0.84	15.75	173.05
Wyoming	11.67	60.96	171.25
Indiana	2.49	16.42	159.42
Arkansas	5.56	33.24	159.15
Nebraska	2.63	19.91	158.03
Mississippi	9.51	32.86	156.21
Iowa	3.80	23.00	152.29
North Dakota	6.66	40.41	149.63
Louisiana	8.10	41.31	145.80
Kansas	4.27	23.48	145.09
West Virginia	3.85	35.35	133.53
Texas	6.87	25.50	121.63
Oklahoma	5.77	28.04	104.37

Here are the top five MSAs in terms of percentage price increases for the year and five years ended March 31, 2007. There are no data for price changes since 1980, so I have ranked them by their five-year totals.

MSA	1-Year	5-Year
Bakersfield, California	3.83	135.67
Maderea, California	3.21	133.30
Miami–Miami Beach– Kendall, Florida	11.44	131.30
Riverside–San Bernardino– Ontario, California	4.14	129.94
Los Angeles–Long Beach– Glendale, California	4.82	124.50

Here are the MSAs with the lowest rates of appreciation for the five-year period.

MSA	1-Year	5-Year
Anderson, Indiana	−0.60	5.12
Kokomo, Indiana	−1.38	6.16
Lafayette, Indiana	3.71	8.18
Detroit–Livonia–Dearborn, Michigan	−2.99	8.55
Flint, Michigan	−2.28	10.50

While all these statistics for home values around the country are interesting, in the end they are just numbers. The number that really counts is the amount you sell your home for minus the real estate agent's fee and what you owe on the mortgage: the dollars you can walk away with.

The point is to have this walk-away amount be enough for you to buy another home free and clear—or mostly so—in a less expensive area, like the Taaffe family in chapter 4. Or, if you are at least sixty-two and want to stay put, you can take out a reverse mortgage on your home. Whichever path you select, you are using your home to make retirement work. Remember, it's your money locked up in that house. Use it to achieve your goals.

Need More Examples?

Let's look at a couple more examples, one hypothetical and one real, of what I'm talking about.

Suppose you live in San Francisco and plan to retire to Las Cruces in southern New Mexico, a popular retirement city that is praised for its climate. Let's assume a preretirement income of $100,000, certainly not unreasonable for a working couple in what are most likely the peak earning years. Let's also assume that you will move from a median-priced house in the San Francisco area that is paid for to a median-priced home in Las Cruces.

First, according to BestPlaces.net, you will need to plan for only $42,718 a year to maintain the same standard of living in Las Cruces that you had on the $100,000 income in San Francisco. In other words, it is 57.3 percent cheaper to live in Las Cruces than in San Francisco. As always, that comparison assumes a mortgage and work-related expenses. Without those, it is cheaper still.

The 2007 median price of a home in San Francisco was $750,000. The median price of a home in Las Cruces was $145,800, well below the national average of $217,200. That means if you sell the San Francisco home and pay a 5 percent real estate broker's fee of $37,500, you can walk away with $712,500. Suppose you use $200,000 of that to move to Las Cruces and buy a home. That leaves $512,500. At 6 percent, that amount would yield an annual income of $30,750, without ever touching the principal; at 4 percent, it would yield $20,500 annually. The property tax rate is higher in Las Cruces than in San Francisco, but the total paid would be much less because of the difference in home values. Almost every other category of expense is cheaper in Las Cruces.

The second example is from real life—mine.

Although I'm a couple of years too old to be counted among the baby boomers, who were born between 1946 and 1964, my 2004 move to a less expensive area—although not to retire in the traditional sense—is illustrative of the power that real estate and location can have on boomer finances.

In May 2004, when I turned sixty, I became eligible for early retirement from the *New York Times*, where I had worked for twelve years as a business editor and columnist. A few weeks earlier I had been offered the R.M. Seaton Professional Journalism Chair at the A.Q. Miller School of Journalism and Mass Communications at Kansas State University in Manhattan, Kansas. After several days of soul-searching and numbers crunching, I decided to trade one Manhattan for another.

At the time, the salary offered in Kansas was $30,000 a year less than I was making at the *Times*, but only $5,000 less than a teaching job I had considered applying for at a New York City university. But the cost of living was 41 percent less expensive in the midwestern Manhattan, according to BestPlaces.net. In reality, then, the lesser salary represented a raise. One example of the difference in the cost of living: insurance for two cars fell to about $800 a year from about $3,000.

Real estate, however, proved to be the plum. My wife, Evelyn, and I had purchased a home in Montclair, New Jersey, in 1993 for $183,000. Along with other areas of the country, especially on the coasts, Montclair—which is very convenient for commuting into New York—experienced rapid increases in property values in the 1990s and early 2000s. We sold our modest house for $434,000, which enabled us to pay off the balance of about $174,000 on the New Jersey mortgage and buy a much larger, and newer, four-bedroom, three-bath house in Kansas for just under $200,000, free and clear. The absence of a mortgage payment was effectively an increase in salary, too. In addition, our property taxes dropped to about $2,700 a year in Kansas from almost $9,000 a year in New Jersey. At the time, according to BestPlaces.net, the median value of a home in Manhattan, Kansas, was $114,900; in Montclair, it was $493,800. The national average was $170,800.

While the move to Kansas was a financial plus, some of our New York friends seemed to think we were falling into a black hole somewhere west of the Hudson River. Living in a university town, however, has many of the cultural pleasures of a big city without the hassles or expense. It's no wonder that such towns—the previously mentioned Oxford, Mississippi, or Bloomington, Indiana, are two examples—are proving so attractive to retirees.

To Renovate or Not

I am often puzzled when I hear people who are planning to sell their homes talking about first remodeling or making some fairly major repairs—like giving the kitchen a makeover or adding a bathroom. You often hear comments like, "Well, you know, if you put in another bathroom, you'll get 90 percent of the cost back when you sell the house." Think about that. If I suggested you give me $10,000 and then in a few months or a year I would give you back $9,000, you'd think I was crazy. But that's exactly what you're doing if you add a $10,000 bathroom to a house you plan to sell soon and get back 90 percent of the cost.

Even if you were to get back 100 percent, what's the point? That would be like investing the $10,000 at zero interest. Some improvements might make a house sell faster ("curb appeal," some real estate agents call it) or make it appeal to a broader group of buyers. But it is going to cost you money, all of which you may not get back.

However, doing work on a house that you plan to live in for, say five to ten years, might make sense. In that case, you'd be getting the use of and pleasure from the improvements, plus the appreciation of the house over the years might well allow you to recoup the repair costs, or even more.

Another mistake is to overimprove a house beyond what is normal for a neighborhood. It could be very difficult to sell the house for enough money to get back even a high percentage of your costs.

Houses on my street sell within a price range that does not vary all that much—no matter what improvements have been made. To get a sense for the price range in your neighborhood, you no longer need to become a real estate spy. Web sites like PropertyShark.com and Zillow.com collect the data for most urban areas.

To build or improve beyond the neighborhood norm might be more reasonable if you plan to stay in your house forever. Then you don't have to be concerned about getting your money back. I have friends who have turned their Victorian home into a showplace far beyond most houses in their area. They have used the best and most expensive materials, including custom-made components. They have no plans to sell their house, however, and expect to enjoy it for the rest of their lives. That makes sense from a personal satisfaction point of view.

But if you're planning to sell your house relatively soon, think hard about putting money into improvements A new roof or a new paint job may move the house faster, but is it worth it? You also run the risk of selecting a color that may not appeal to some buyers. Maybe it would be better to take a month or so longer to sell the house as it is. Or drop the asking price a bit and explain that this is to allow the buyer to do his or her own painting or reroofing.

There are exceptions. Your house, for instance, has to be in working order. It would be tough to sell a home with a broken heating system. If your wall-to-wall carpets are worn and dirty—and they are covering hardwood floors—it might pay to spend $1,000 to $2,000 to take up the carpets and refinish the floors. An improvement like that might pay for itself and then some.

Seek the advice of an independent home appraiser on such matters. Also, there are many organizations and publications that have lists showing what percentage of a home remodeling or repair investment you can expect to get back when you sell your house. A good place to check for such information is *Smart Money* magazine's Web site (www.smartmoney.com).

Be aware, though, that these payback estimates are all over the place and even vary within a given city or region. Many of the lists estimate that you will get back 90 to 100 percent for things like adding a bathroom, remodeling a kitchen, or adding a new heating system. On the other hand, you're likely to get back only 15 to 60 percent for finishing a basement, adding a swimming pool, or upgrading the landscaping.

An article on real estate myths by Vivian Marino in the April 8, 2007, issue of *PARADE* magazine suggested a cost-effective alternative to remodeling. "A less expensive strategy is to 'stage' a home, creating a neutral setting that appeals to a range of tastes," she wrote. "The goal is to draw attention to a home's merits and minimize its shortcomings." Long a staple of buyer-driven real estate markets, this will likely entail that simplifying garage sale *before* you put your house up for sale. Pack up your mementos and knickknacks and spend $100 or so on beige bedspreads that you can throw over more colorful choices that match your style—but possibly not every buyer's. That's a lot less than spending $20,000 to remodel a bathroom.

So if you're planning to sell your house and retire, carefully assess any money you're considering spending for repairs or redecorating. You may not get it back. Remember: cutting expenses increases income.

REVERSE MORTGAGES: A THIRD WAY

A surprising number of people have never heard of reverse mortgages or have only the vaguest idea about them.

AARP points out on its excellent reverse mortgage Web site (www.aarp.org/revmort) that until the beginning of federally insured reverse mortgages in 1989, there were only two main ways to get cash—an owner's equity—out of a house. You could sell it, but then you would have to move. Or you could borrow against the value of your home, but that meant monthly payments to repay the loans. And if for some reason you couldn't make those monthly payments, you would risk losing your house—the collateral for the loan.

AARP was one of the prime forces in getting federal legislation passed to insure reverse mortgages—thus allowing what the group calls "a third way" of getting money from your home without leaving it or facing monthly payments.

The concept of a reverse mortgage, or home-equity conversion, is simple: you borrow against your home's value, but you are not re- quired to make any repayments of principal or interest as long as you stay put. The amount you owe will grow larger—and your equity will shrink—as time goes by because you are making no payments. It's the reverse of a conventional mortgage in which your debt de- clines and your equity rises as you make payments. If you move or die with a reverse mortgage, you or your heirs must pay back the loan, including interest and charges, usually by selling the house. In the meantime, no one can kick you out as long as your pay your property taxes and homeowners insurance and maintain the house.

Here's a really good part: if you live long enough for the accumu- lating interest to push the total debt above your home's value, the dif- ference is paid by insurance that is built into the loan. That means the mortgage company can't touch anything else in your estate. This is known as a nonrecourse loan. In other words, a lender's only recourse for getting the loan repaid is the value of the home in question.

You can receive the proceeds, which are generally not subject to taxes, from a reverse mortgage in several ways:

- As a credit line, with either a fixed limit or a limit whose balance will increase each year equal to the interest rate you are charged.
- In a lump-sum cash payment.
- In monthly payments for a specified number of years or as long as you live in your home.

You're not stuck with one choice. The payment options can be blended or even changed later.

If you take the lump-sum cash payment, you could invest the proceeds in an annuity that would provide monthly payments to you for the rest of your life, no matter where you live.

Martha York, a widow in Port St. Lucie, Florida, needed to sup- plement her monthly income of about $1,200 from Social Security and an annuity. In 1998, when she was seventy-five, she took out a reverse mortgage on her home, then valued at $80,000. She elected to take a combination of a $5,000 lump-sum payment and $300 a month for life. This boosted her monthly income by 25 percent, to $1,500. She has been pleased with her decision, which also allowed her to make some improvements to her home. "It's a terrific thing," she said. "I intend to live long enough to use up all the value in my house and then some."

In 2003, Peter and Ruth Ricca of Metairie, Louisiana, took out a reverse mortgage on their home to, as Ruth Ricca put it, "give us a pad, an extra bit of money to make us feel comfortable." She was seventy-eight; he was eighty. The two had retired from the grocery and restaurant business more than a decade and a half earlier as they had each turned sixty-two. They had only their Social Security benefits and savings to live on. When they applied for the reverse mortgage, their house was valued at $230,000. They elected to take a lump-sum payment of $105,000. They used $15,000 of that to pay off a bank loan and used another $15,000 to pay some additional bills. The remaining $75,000 they put away to be used as necessary. "We're very happy with the arrangement," Ruth said.

Help from HUD

While the concept behind reverse mortgages is simple, they have many variations and the details are complex. Over the years, this has led some borrowers to turn unnecessarily to outside agents, who have charged fees of up to 10 percent of a loan for "referral" services and information that is available free from the government and other sources.

That's one reason the Department of Housing and Urban Development, the primary insurer of reverse mortgages, requires consumers to confer with HUD-approved counselors before getting these federally insured loans. The only fees you should ever pay are regular loan application and origination fees—directly to the lender. These fees do not have to be paid up front. They can become a part of the loan.

To qualify, homeowners must be sixty-two. Obviously, you must have equity in your home, but it does not have to be fully paid for. There are no income requirements. Mobile homes are not eligible, although modular and manufactured homes are okay if they are permanent and taxed as real estate, not motor vehicles.

Condominiums are also eligible for the federally insured loans, although cooperative apartments are not. Ken Scholen, a reverse mortgage specialist with AARP, says HUD is moving to make co-ops eligible. The difficulty with co-ops is that owners do not own their homes directly, but instead own shares in an entity that owns their property. One lender, Financial Freedom in Irvine, California, has a pilot program for co-op reverse mortgages in New York City. Because they are not federally insured, these mortgages cost a bit more, but they are still nonrecourse loans and all the other rules and safeguards apply.

The interest rates charged for federally insured reverse mortgages are adjustable and based on the one-year Treasury rate. "Generally, annually adjustable reverse mortgage rates will be a bit less than rates for an annually adjustable forward, or conventional, mortgage," Scholen said. Federally insured reverse mortgages—under a program called Home Equity Conversion Mortgage, or HECM— are by far the most popular, accounting for more than 90 percent of all such loans.

Scholen offered a bit of timely advice in 2007 for those considering a reverse mortgage: wait a year or two if possible. "Rates and fees for reverse mortgages have been pretty much the same for a long time," he explained. "But now, as they are becoming more popular, there is increased competition in rates and fees. Unless it's an emergency, wait a year or two. You'll get a better deal as lenders push for lower prices and more choices."

Is It for You?

In 2005, the National Council on Aging released a report showing that 13 million Americans were eligible for reverse mortgages. The amount you can borrow through a federally insured reverse mortgage is limited, regardless of your home's value, and varies from state to state and even from county to county. The AARP reverse mortgage Web site has a calculator that will tell you how much you can borrow based on your home's value, your age, and where you live. If you owe money on your home, generally you must pay off the loan with the money you get from the reverse mortgage. The older you are, the more you can borrow. At the Web site you can also download, order online, or order by telephone a free AARP book titled *Home Made Money: A Consumer's Guide to Reverse Mortgages.*

Keep in mind that even though you can have a reverse mortgage and live in your house as long as you want, the loan must be paid off when you move or die. If you want to leave your home free and clear to your children, then a reverse mortgage may not be for you. Also, because of the loan fees and charges, a reverse mortgage is more expensive in the early years of the loan. Therefore, it's a bad idea to take out a reverse mortgage if you plan to sell your house anytime soon.

You don't have to be pressed for cash to get a reverse mortgage.

Aleck and Sheila Townsley are comfortably retired in Foster City, California, in a house that overlooks San Francisco Bay. They are able to live well on retirement incomes from his career as a lawyer and hers as a teacher. But in 1999, when they were both sixty-five, they used their home—then valued at $555,000—for a reverse mortgage. They chose a $65,000 line of credit that would eventually grow to $170,000 so they could afford "extras" like travel. "I have no children," Aleck Townsley said. "I want to spend my last dime with my last breath."

The advantages of a reverse mortgage are clear if you want to stay in your current home when you retire. Such a loan can also be helpful even if you plan to sell your home and use the equity to pay cash for another house in a less expensive area. In the hypothetical case of Joe and Sue Sample in chapter 2, they could sell their house in the New York area and be able to pay cash for a home in Tucson, Arizona. When they are old enough to qualify, they could easily take out a reverse mortgage on the Arizona home. In one sense, they would be getting the best of both worlds since the proceeds from a reverse mortgage represent only a portion of the equity in a home. The Samples would get all their equity, $330,000, out of their East Coast house. The Tucson home might cost $210,000. A reverse mortgage on the new home would be gravy on top of the equity realized from the first house.

If you are sixty-two and find yourself house rich and cash poor, a reverse mortgage could be an important part of your retirement plans.

In September 2002, Kathleen Maddox, a widow in Billings, Montana, turned sixty-two. That same month she applied for a reverse mortgage. "I did it right away, as soon as I was sixty-two and eligible," she said. "I was pretty low on money." Her husband had died ten years earlier and she had been a homemaker most of her life except for part-time work in the schools her four children attended.

Her home was valued at $118,000, and she selected a reverse mortgage that provided her with a $41,000 line of credit. The balance in her line of credit will grow each year at a rate equal to the interest she is being charged for the reverse mortgage. Maddox planned to use some of the money for repairs on her house, and was considering buying a used, but newer, car. She is also doing some traveling for her "mental health." She is the sole caregiver for a ninety-two-year-old mother. "It was time for me to have a break," she said. The Thanksgiving after she got the loan, Maddox went to Phoenix to visit a sister for two weeks. Then at Christmas she visited another sister in North Dakota. She is pleased with how things have worked out. Her grown children—a daughter in Seattle and three sons in the Billings area—had no objections when she decided on a reverse mortgage. "They told me, 'If that's what you want to do, Mom, go for it,'" she said.

ABOUT THAT SLUMP

It's no wonder that two years of doom-and-gloom news about the housing market has rattled buyers and sellers—not to mention prospective retirees. As sales and prices have retreated from record highs, one widely quoted economist predicted that a collapsing housing market "bubble" would drag the economy into a "much nastier, deeper and more protracted" recession than the one in 2001.

But Blanche Evans, the editor of RealtyTimes.com and the author of *Bubbles, Booms, and Busts: Making Money in Any Real Estate Market* (McGraw-Hill, 2006), isn't buying it. She sees the slump that began in 2006 as more of a breather, as well as a chance for buyers and sellers to "reposition" themselves to take advantage of the long-term upward trend in housing prices. In other words, she contends there's money to be made in real estate even if prices head south for a while.

Evans argues that the most recent slump has mainly forced a lot of quick-money speculators—so-called flippers—out of the housing market. "In the normal market, people are still buying and selling homes," she said. "The market is not crashing; the fundamentals and incentives are still extremely good for everyone else."

News reports have tended to support her judgment. In the spring of 2007, both CNN and the Associated Press reported on disappearing flippers, those investors who buy homes and hope to resell them for a quick profit in areas of rapid appreciation. According to CNN, investment-home sales fell 28.9 percent in 2006, while vacation-home sales—driven by lifestyle choices instead of speculation—actually rose by 4.7 percent during the year. The AP reported that many speculators in the Las Vegas, Nevada, area were left "upside down," or owing more on their mortgages than their homes were worth. As a result, the lines those flippers used to form outside home-building companies' sales offices have disappeared.

Even if there is a prolonged recession in the housing market, Evans expects it to be relatively mild on a national level. "One reason for all the pessimism is that the financial press often assumes that whatever is happening on the coasts is happening to the rest of the country," she said. "But the Midwest, for example, may not experience the highs and lows of the coastal cities."

For buyers, sagging prices present an opportunity to acquire a more desirable home. "You can get a better price on a better home that will pay off when the slump ends," she said. Interest rates, of course, can be a factor—along with the possibility that a house you buy in a falling market may continue to drop in value. Evans points out, however, that mortgages can be refinanced to take advantage of better rates, and recessions traditionally last only a couple of years.

For sellers, she emphasizes that the most important factor is how long they have owned their homes. "You may not make as much, but if you've owned your home for several years, you're still going to make money," she said. Or, if you have the financial flexibility, you can rent your house until the market improves.

As for regional differences in home prices, she argues that what seems to be overinflated values in some parts of the country—the San Francisco Bay area, for example—have more to do with desirability than affordability. "If pricing were just about affordability for the average person, homes in these areas would not be nearly so high," she said. "What's driving these prices is the idea that a home in a location like San Francisco is a good buy even though the price is high. It's expected to go higher because this is an area where people want to live."

She added: "This is all about improving your position. When things are bad, they're not bad for everybody; they may not be bad for you. That's when you should improve your position. Buy, sell, or hold. It's a poker game."

WHAT ABOUT RENTING?

As home prices and sales have declined since 2006, there have been a number of articles in newspapers and magazines suggesting that renting instead of buying might be the way to go until the housing market improves.

Perhaps. But people contemplating retirement should take two factors into consideration: lifestyle and how long they expect to be retired. Renting can be a hassle, with less space, less privacy, and noisy neighbors. It also means the expense of another move if you are waiting for a real estate upturn. My advice is to think long term. And, in the long term, renting doesn't make a lot of sense.

A decline in home prices might actually be a good thing overall. One result of high prices is that many people simply have been priced out of the market in places like New York and San Francisco. An article in the *New York Times* at the height of the housing boom in 2005 cited potential home buyers simply giving up in the face of average sales prices for Manhattan apartments that were approaching $1 million. The monthly payments on a thirty-year mortgage for $1 million at a rate of 6.5 percent would be $6,320 a month. A $750,000 mortgage would mean payments of $4,740 a month. These figures don't include taxes and other expenses like condo fees or co-op maintenance charges. With prices like these, paying $2,000 a month for rent might not look so bad.

The reality, however, is that renting—and building no equity in a home—is unlikely to be a money-saving move. Of course, as we have seen, housing prices can fall in the short term. Over the long haul, however, it's hard to make a case against home ownership. Mortgage interest, which is most of a mortgage payment for many years, and property taxes are deductible from your income taxes; rent is not. If you buy and have a fixed-rate mortgage, you have stabilized much of your housing costs no matter what happens to inflation and the rental market. Your house, in which you are building equity, is almost certain to increase in value over the years—maybe a lot, depending on location; rent builds no equity. Even if the home you buy doesn't rise in value as rapidly as in the past or as rapidly as property in more desirable areas, you'll still be better off than having paid rent. When you retire, you'll be able to sell your home and use the profit to buy another one mortgage-free in a less expensive area. Not so if you have been renting. Even once you're retired, renting doesn't make sense for many of the same reasons. Why not continue to build equity that you may need someday if you require, say, assisted living?

THINKING IN STAGES

It's important to remember as you consider retirement and real estate—or retirement and anything else, for that matter—that there are few rules and nothing is forever. You can and may change your mind.

Especially since the boomers have come on the scene, there has been a lot of talk about the "stages" of retirement. In 2006, *USA Today* ran an article about the "five stages" for "hearty boomers," including a phase of planning for retirement that Ken Dychtwald calls the "imagination" phase, which starts about fifteen years before actual retirement. Citing him and others, the article went on to run down the "anticipation" stage, which comes about five years before actual retirement; the "implementation" stage, which comes in the first couple of years of retirement; and two later stages, "reorientation" and "final," which don't sound nearly as enticing but seem to make up the bulk of the traditional retirement years. In earlier generations, the article said, retirement had only two stages: "go" and "no go."

It's true that as our life spans have increased, so too have the years we will spend in retirement. A boomer who lives to be ninety could end up spending a third of his or her life "retired" in some way. According to most thinking, more years must equal more stages.

The problem, however, is that life and retirement—whatever that turns out to be for you—are far too complex to fall neatly into five artificial stages. I know a woman in Kansas named Helen Brockman who lives unassisted in her own home at the age of 105; she has had more careers than *USA Today* has stages. Before "retiring" as a teacher of fashion design at Kansas State University, she worked as a fashion designer in New York. It was there, in 1965, that she published *The Theory of Fashion Design* (John Wiley and Sons), an authoritative textbook that made her name widely known in the industry. In 2005, she published a 582-page autobiography, *Both Sides of Nice* (KS Publications), and is currently working on a book about astrology. What stage is she in? Then, of course, we all know people in their thirties and forties who live like they're in one of the later stages identified in the *USA Today* article.

Nevertheless, as you move into retirement, it's wise to think not so much in terms of "stages" but in commonsense terms of how much responsibility you will want to continue to shoulder—or be able to shoulder—in the future. Issues like downsizing, real estate choices, reverse mortgages, and ease of living come into play, and they may not fit precisely into any phase. You may want an easy-to-maintain and easy-to-lock-and-leave condo so you can take off hiking in the Rockies. It may come in handy later when you're no longer able to clean your gutters. Keeping the future in mind means you might take that one-floor condo instead of a three-story town house so that you're not someday cursing those stairs or forced to move. You may decide to take out a reverse mortgage to help with living expenses or to fund travel. Which stage does that fit in?

There's nothing wrong with planning for the future. But don't get trapped there, or in someone else's notion of a phase or stage. The actor Orson Bean, not long after he had spent his seventy-fifth birthday at a Club Med in Mexico, said to me in an interview: "I made the discovery, it's always now. It's now and three seconds from now is still now."

6

Key No. 2: Your Health Insurance

Trying to buy an individual policy is tough; thirty to forty
percent of the people we try to place are getting turned down.
—STEPHEN L. WYSS, MANAGING DIRECTOR
OF AFFINITY GROUP UNDERWRITERS

Health insurance is vital to your retirement plans. Without it, you risk losing everything. The United States is one of the few nations without some form of national health insurance regardless of your age, where you work, or whether you work at all. Universal coverage in this country—Medicare—is offered only to those sixty-five or older. If you want to retire before you are sixty-five, you're on your own for health insurance. Many people in this fix are rejected for individual health policies because of preexisting conditions; those healthy enough to qualify for coverage sometimes can't afford the premiums. For many, the only alternative—an expensive alternative—is to extend their employer coverage under a federal law called COBRA and when that expires switch to coverage—also expensive—under another federal law called HIPAA. We'll look at both alternatives in this chapter.

Some people are lucky. They work for companies that provide health benefits for retirees, although sometimes at a steep price. But at least the insurance is available and covers preexisting conditions, which is vital. Employer-provided retiree coverage, however, is a shrinking benefit. Less than a third of companies now offer it, according to a survey by the Mercer Health and Benefits consulting firm. In 1993, almost half did. Moreover, only 18 percent of large employers contribute to the cost of health benefits for retirees younger than sixty-five. This is down from 30 percent in 1993.

These numbers represent a big problem for many people in their mid-fifties and early sixties. You don't have to spend much time talking to people in that age group in today's high-stress workforce to learn that the urge to retire early is pervasive. Many want an early exit, but not without health insurance. They rightly fear that one serious illness could wipe them out financially.

The high price of many prescription drugs makes getting prescription coverage an important element of your health insurance plan in retirement, particularly if you require expensive brand-name medicines. In that case, you should shop for insurance plans that include such coverage. Once you are eligible for Medicare, you will also be eligible for drug coverage through what is called Medicare Part D.

I believe that many people can figure out ways to affordably get health insurance and prescription drug coverage, although it isn't always easy. With a little care and attention, it is possible to maintain health insurance throughout your retirement.

INSURANCE FOR YOUR HEALTH

The biggest health insurance challenge hits people who have no retiree coverage through their jobs and are forced to purchase individual insurance, which can carry high prices and harsh limitations on preexisting conditions. Insurance companies in all but a few states can exclude from coverage any health problems related to preexisting conditions or even refuse to cover you. This is especially a problem for people in their fifties, who are much more likely to have preexisting conditions than people, say, in their twenties or thirties.

Your access to an individual policy depends in large part on the state of your finances, the state of your health, and the state where you live. The states have varying laws that govern access to individual health insurance. The first step in shopping for an individual policy is finding out if you live in a state with a *guaranteed-issue law* or *community rating*. Guaranteed-issue laws require that any insurance companies offering individual policies to residents in the state have to sell you insurance regardless of your preexisting conditions. As of 2007, four states carry these laws: Maine, New Jersey, New York, and Vermont. (Massachusetts, which used to be in this group, now has mandatory universal coverage.) Because insurers in these states have to take all comers, regardless of health conditions, the policies are comparatively expensive, and there can be waiting periods before coverage becomes active for people who do not have prior insurance. The higher premiums put insurance out of reach for some people. Guaranteed issue doesn't mean guaranteed affordability.

If you are healthy and have no preexisting medical conditions, buying individual insurance should not be difficult in a state without guaranteed-issue laws. It will certainly be less expensive. Insurance underwriters, however, are very risk-averse whenever they are allowed to be, so they will look for any opening to exclude a preexisting condition and perhaps deny you coverage altogether. That allows insurers to cover only people at low risk for getting sick, a practice called *cherry-picking.* "Trying to buy an individual policy is tough; thirty to forty percent of the people we try to place are getting turned down," said Stephen L. Wyss, the managing director of Affinity Group Underwriters. If an insurer agrees to cover you but excludes a preexisting condition from the coverage, shop around. A policy that doesn't cover a stroke or heart disease because you have high blood pressure probably won't be worth the premiums.

The good news is that although state laws governing insurance vary widely, generally once you are issued a policy it can't be canceled unless your insurer stops doing business in your state. Also, you generally cannot be singled out for a rate increase if you develop a health problem; rates must be increased for your entire "class," which usually refers to people in your age group but can include other groupings like geography. A very helpful Web site run by the Georgetown University Health Policy Institute (www.healthinsuranceinfo.net) can provide you with current information on insurance rules in various states.

The other major consideration in buying an individual policy is community rating. Most states allow insurers to base the initial premiums charged for individual policies on a client's health and age. The four "guaranteed-issue" states—Maine, New Jersey, New York, and Vermont—have community rating to one degree or another. Insurers in these states must charge all residents the same premium regardless of their health status. In Maine and Vermont there can be limited premium differences depending on your age, occupation, and smoking status. New York and New Jersey have virtually no exceptions that would allow for premium differences. Premiums in these four states are uniform and high, so there are only modest differences among plans offered by rival insurance companies.

If you suffer from preexisting conditions that are closing you out of coverage elsewhere, it may pay to move to a guaranteed-issue state (or Massachusetts) rather than face bankrupting medical costs down the road. By the same token, if you are healthy and live in a guaranteed-issue state like New York and New Jersey where individual premiums are high, you could move to a nearby state with less expensive premiums. Premiums in Pennsylvania and Delaware, for example, are much less than in New Jersey; Connecticut is less than New York. Either way, it doesn't have to be a big move if you live near the border of one of these states. The expense of an occasional trip to visit relatives or friends where you used to live could be more than offset by the savings on insurance premiums.

If you want to retire early but must buy individual coverage, you need to pick the best coverage for your personal situation. The first step involves determining how your preexisting conditions, if you have any, will affect your ability to get insurance. You may need to confirm *credit for prior coverage*, normally with a letter from your former insurer, if you are switching insurance plans and need preexisting conditions covered right away. Then you should identify the type of plan that will best fit your retirement lifestyle and health needs.

A *fee-for-service (indemnity) plan* is the traditional kind of health care policy that allows you to go to any doctor or hospital you choose. Deductibles, the amount you pay before your insurance kicks in, can range from several hundred to several thousand dollars. After you have paid bills totaling your deductible, the plan usually pays 80 percent of all bills; you pay the other 20 percent up to an out-of-pocket maximum that generally runs between $1,500 and $3,000, but can be higher. After you have reached the out-of-pocket maximum, the policy pays 100 percent of your medical expenses. An indemnity plan is usually the most expensive health insurance you can buy but provides the most flexibility in your choice of doctors.

An *HMO (health maintenance organization)* is essentially a pre-paid health plan. For a monthly premium, the HMO provides comprehensive care. You will likely pay a co-payment for office visits, but most HMO plans have no deductibles. There are usually no forms to fill out or bills to keep track of. You are, however, quite limited in your choice of doctors, hospitals, and other health care providers. You commonly must get a referral from your primary care physician to see a specialist; if you don't, your treatment with the specialist won't be covered. HMOs were designed to control costs, and they have been the source of many consumer complaints, ranging from coverage limitations to the fact that some doctors were compensated for denying treatment or referrals to patients while others were punished for providing what was considered by the HMO to be excessive treatment. Because of their comprehensive, deductible-free coverage, HMOs often compete with the most affordable health-insurance options. Be wary, however, if you plan to travel a lot or move after you retire. Payment for medical expenses outside the coverage area of many HMOs can be limited to emergency care only.

A *PPO (preferred provider organization) plan* is a cross between a fee-for-service plan and an HMO. You can see any doctor you choose without a referral, although if the physician is outside the insurance plan's network you will probably be reimbursed at a lower rate. For network doctors, you usually have only a co-payment for office visits. There can be varying co-payments—as well as deductibles, coinsurance, and out-of-pocket maximums—depending on the policy. A *POS (point-of-service) plan* is like a PPO except that you need a referral from your primary care physician to see an out-of-network doctor, for which you may have to pay extra. Without the referral, you will likely have to pay the entire bill for the out-of-network physician. A PPO or POS plan can be a good compromise for someone looking for affordable coverage that extends beyond one local area.

If your primary concern is protection against the financial shock that can result from a serious illness or accident, there are several guidelines you should follow.

- **Look for a policy with a low stop-loss.** The out-of-pocket maximum is the amount you must pay yourself before an insurance policy will pay 100 percent of your bills; the out-of-pocket maximum may or may not include the deductible. The term *stop-loss* is sometimes used to refer to the point at which you have met your deductible and paid your out-of-pocket maximum. Stop-loss amounts can vary from as little as $1,200 to many thousands of dollars.
- **Consider a policy with a high lifetime maximum,** which is the maximum amount of covered expenses your insurance company will pay in your lifetime. Look for a policy with a lifetime maximum of at least $3 million. A million dollars, which is the cap on some policies, may sound like a lot of money, but at today's exploding medical prices it's possible for a single major illness or two to eat that up.
- **Get secondary coverage if possible.** If both you and your spouse are retiring and you both have retiree group health insurance benefits through your jobs, each can probably take the insurance and list the other as a dependent. You won't receive double payments for medical bills, but each of you will have secondary coverage that will usually pay the part of a medical bill not paid by the primary insurer. This is

known as *coordination of benefits* and usually works only with employer-based group coverage. Such a strategy may cost you more each month in premiums but can really pay off in the event of a major illness or accident. Of course, if one of your policies is a really good one that covers most everything, double coverage may be a waste of money.

- **Watch out for fine-print limits** on certain things like chemotherapy, physical therapy, and home health care, where some insurance companies try to cut corners on coverage.
- **Avoid policies with payment caps on specific medical and surgical procedures**. Limited benefit plans have set amounts they will pay for things like surgeries and hospital room and board. These polices are less expensive but could leave you woefully underinsured for a major illness or accident. Also watch out for limitations on regular polices. Some, for instance, will have unrealistically low caps on certain surgeries or medical procedures. One example: a $50,000 limit for organ-transplant surgery. Such surgery can cost four to five times that, or more.

HEALTH SAVINGS ACCOUNTS

If, on the other hand, you have enough savings to cover the out-of-pocket expenses of a serious illness or accident—which can amount to thousands of dollars—you should consider a high-deductible, or catastrophic, policy, perhaps one linked to a health savings account, or HSA. An HSA policy is linked to a tax-free savings account that can be used to pay medical bills before you meet the policy's deductible. You might, for example, be less concerned about coverage for things like doctor visits. Instead of having a *co-payment*, a flat fee usually in the range of $10 to $30 that you pay for each health care service, you would pay for services until you reached your policy's deductible. While you may seem to be paying more for your care, your premiums could be reduced by as much as 40 percent or more.

HSAs are the most visible result of a push by the George W. Bush administration and the former Republican Congress toward consumer-directed, or consumer-driven, health care. Consumer-directed health care is supposed to lower the cost to companies of providing employee health coverage and to help individuals who must buy their own insurance.

HSAs were born of a conviction that market forces will trigger improved health care and lower prices as patients, forced to spend their own money, negotiate for the best deal and use the health care system sparingly. The problem with this argument is that buying health care is not like buying a car or a refrigerator. Prices are not posted and doctors rarely discuss their charges; mere mortals cannot hope to comprehend the dizzying and inconsistent list of hospital charges. Advocates of HSAs and consumer-driven health care, of course, argue that if HSAs become the way most people get health care, the medical pricing system will be forced to become more transparent. In fact, a few large physician groups have begun posting prices for many procedures.

Although HSAs don't solve the big problems facing the health care system, they do have the potential to make health insurance less expensive for some people. Unfortunately, individual HSAs do nothing for the problem of people who can't get insurance because of preexisting conditions. That's too bad, because HSAs are ideal for retirees, who would benefit from the low premiums and probably have enough money to easily fund the linked accounts.

An HSA must be established in conjunction with the purchase of a catastrophic health insurance policy that carries a high deductible and is thus cheaper than traditional coverage. Money you put in an HSA each year is tax-free and can be used for payments toward your health insurance deductibles. You may not, however, use the money in the account to pay your health policy premiums. Plus, if you use the money you contribute to the plan or any of the investment income the money earns for anything but medical expenses, you must pay taxes and a 10 percent penalty on the amount withdrawn. The account balance can build year to year.

When you turn sixty-five and become eligible for Medicare, you can use the HSA funds for anything you want; if, at that point, you spend the money on nonmedical expenses, however, you must pay taxes on it (but not the penalty). If you spend it on medical expenses, the money remains free from federal taxes. The funds are also free from state taxes in most states. Of the forty-three states that have some form of income tax, as of this writing there are seven that tax contributions to HSAs: Alabama, California, Maine, Massachusetts, New Jersey, Pennsylvania, and Wisconsin.

For individuals, insurance plans must have an annual deductible of $1,100 or more to be eligible for a companion health savings account; for families, the deductible must be $2,200 or more. As of 2007, individuals could make a contribution to their HSA in any amount up to $2,850 for an individual and $5,650 for a family. These and other limits are inflation-indexed and will increase. If you are over fifty-five when you establish an HSA, you can make an additional catch-up contribution of $900 each year; this will increase to $1,000 in 2009. If your insurance has a higher deductible than the annual limit, the difference is your responsibility. The yearly inflation-indexed out-of-pocket maximum, however, is $5,500 for an individual and $11,000 for a family, regardless of your catastrophic plan; these maximums include deductibles and any co-payments or coinsurance you must pay.

"Ideally, the deductible on your policy would match the maximum on your HSA, but there could be a gap if you picked a higher deductible policy," said Robert Hurley, the chief operating officer for Health Savings Account Solutions at the big online health insurance broker eHealthInsurance.com, which is aggressively pushing individual HSA-eligible policies. "But since the account builds year to year, that gap will disappear. I recommend buying a policy with a deductible that matches your HSA, then increase the deductible—and lower your premiums—as your savings build."

Setting Up an HSA

Let's consider the Samples from chapter 2 again. This time let's assume that Joe's employer didn't provide retiree health insurance and he needed to purchase it on his own. The two plan to retire in a few months when they are sixty; both are in good health and able to qualify for an HSA. They find an HSA-eligible plan with premiums of $325 a month and a deductible of $5,650. They contribute $5,650 a year, or $471 a month, to their linked account. They assume they'll spend a total of $2,000 a year on health care until they are sixty-five and become eligible for Medicare. After one year, they will have $3,650 left in the account, to which they can add another $5,650 the second year and so on for five years. During that period they will have spent $10,000 on medical expenses, none of it covered by their policy because of the high deductible, and $19,500 on premiums— a total of $29,500. Assuming a return of 6.5 percent, they will have saved $33,303 in the linked account, plus whatever they saved by not paying taxes on their contributions. So they will come out ahead. For a traditional policy, their premiums alone would have totaled $30,000 to $40,000, or even more, without accounting for co-payments, and they would not have had the tax-free savings. Chapter 9 contains worksheets that can help you sort out this and other medical expense problems.

Another advantage of an HSA is that you can use the money to pay for health-related expenses that insurance may not cover. These can include weight-loss and smoking-cessation programs, as well as premiums for long-term care insurance. In addition, many of these plans pay 100 percent of medical bills after the deductible has been met, with no co-payments.

HSAs are available in most states and will eventually be available in all. One holdup is that some state laws and regulations must be tweaked or repealed to allow HSA-eligible policies. Another holdup is that insurance companies have simply not designed HSA policies for a few of the states.

At the end of 2006, there were 3.6 million health savings accounts, although the *Wall Street Journal* reported in June 2007 that their growth was beginning to falter because of low satisfaction with some of the plans. The fact is, HSAs aren't for everyone. Critics argue that the tax benefits of the plans favor higher-income people who can afford to fund the accounts and those with good health, usually younger people, whose accounts can build and exceed the deductibles. There are also concerns that as healthy workers switch to HSAs, the cost of traditional plans for older workers will increase—there will be fewer younger people in non-HSA plans to subsidize the care of older, less healthy employees.

At eHealthInsurance.com, visitors can anonymously get instant premium quotes and compare plans in every state. All you have to provide is your zip code, birth date, gender, number of dependents, whether you are a smoker, and whether you are a student. There are other online brokers that provide premium quotes, but some—like Insure.com—require you to give your name and fill out a health questionnaire.

If you decide to go with an HSA, keep the following points in mind:

- **Make sure you have sufficient income to fund your HSA account** and fully understand what your costs will be. If you can't fund the account, you certainly aren't going to be able to afford the hundreds or thousands of dollars you will have to pay up front if you get sick.
- **Make an assessment of your annual health expenses and the state of your health.** Is there a history of a particular illness in your family to which you might be unusually susceptible that could wipe out your HSA before you qualify for Medicare? Are you the kind of person who might skimp on health care if you have to spend your own money for it? Skipping a visit to the doctor if you have a sinus headache might make sense; waiting to see if a changed skin lesion worsens, or if chest pains are simple indigestion, might not.
- **Look for a policy that pays 100 percent of your medical expenses** after the deductible has been met. Otherwise, you could face thousands of dollars in additional charges. If you're buying coverage on your own, the difference in premiums between policies with 100 percent coverage and those with less is not that great, sometimes as little as $15 a month.

- **Check that a policy has a lifetime maximum of at least $3 million.**
- **Be aware that most HSA policies are linked to PPOs, or preferred provider organizations.** This means that if you choose to go to a doctor or hospital outside the network, you must pay more even if you have met your deductible. (A policy that pays 80 percent after the deductible is met might pay only 60 percent for out-of-network services.)
- **Be aware that HSAs often don't provide prescription drug coverage until you have met your deductible.** Even after you have met the deductible, you may have to pay for the drugs up front and submit the bills to your insurance carrier for reimbursement.
- **Brace yourself for bookkeeping and paperwork hassles.** You'll need to keep copies of bills and payments, as well as file claim forms. Lack of organization and attention to details can cost you money.
- **Understand that the money you put into your health savings account can be at risk,** especially if it's invested in stocks. Watch out for fees charged for the accounts by banks and financial services companies. These can run as much as $45 or more during the first year of a new account.

A Look at Prices

It may seem as though insurance providers make their plans complex specifically so you can't compare them side by side as you would, say, a life insurance policy. To help get a handle on the differences in coverage among various kinds of individual health insurance policies, I visited eHealthInsurance.com to gather some quotes on premiums for three kinds of policies in three cities. The quotes— for a sixty-year-old couple with no children—are for the least expensive premiums for HMO, PPO, and HSA-eligible policies. One of the cities included in the comparisons is in New Jersey, a guaranteed-issue and community-rating state but one where individual HSAs were not yet available. These examples give a snapshot of the cheapest policies available, regardless of the deductible, which can be as high as $10,000. A different comparison, for example by deductibles or benefits, would yield a very different set of prices and ranking. You should decide which elements of a policy are more important to you and shop accordingly. Keep in mind that the prices in this and other chapters will likely have changed by the time this book is published; it is the relative differences among them that will untangle the costs for your own coverage.

Married Sixty-year-old Couple with No Children

	HMO	PPO	HSA
Ocean City, New Jersey	$633.01	$848.80	N.A.
Tucson, Arizona	$699.00	$245.02	$242.05
San Diego, California	$458.00	$414.24	$449.00

If a quick look at these prices leaves you puzzled, don't worry—even health insurance brokers can have trouble sorting them out. In some states, there are more than a hundred different individual policies available. Remember, the comparison is on prices only, not benefits or deductibles. One of the factors affecting price differences from state to state is the degree to which a state mandates coverage. You can see right away the effects that guaranteed-issue laws have on insurance prices in New Jersey. In addition, some states require that certain medical procedures be covered. These mandates may cover basic traditional medical services and provide valuable protections for policyholders; they may also include services like acupuncture, alcohol abuse treatment, or pastoral counseling. The more the mandates, the higher the insurance premiums. The Council for Affordable Health Insurance, an advocacy group for insurers, estimates that state mandates increase the cost of coverage from 20 to 50 percent. You can find an up-to-date list of state mandates at the council's Web site (www.cahi.org).

As you sort through the options, you may want to consult an insurance agent directly. Although eHealthInsurance.com provides quotes online, the company has a toll-free number (1-800-977-8860) you can call for personal assistance. If you feel more comfortable dealing face-to-face with an agent, the National Association of Health Underwriters' Web site (www.nahu.org) can help you find one in your area. Keep in mind that when agents sell an insurance policy, the insurer pays them a broker commission. These commissions vary and some agents may push high-commission policies that are more in their interests than yours. So in the end you may still want to use a source like eHealthInsurance.com to check your options against a policy recommended by an agent.

COBRA AND HIPAA

For most people with preexisting conditions and no employer-sponsored retiree coverage, the easy but expensive way to coverage lies with a federal law known as COBRA, or the Consolidated Omnibus Budget Reconciliation Act. If the company you are leaving has more than twenty employees, the law allows you to continue your employer-provided coverage temporarily, but at your expense. Another federal law also gives you a guarantee of switching from COBRA to an individual insurance plan later. If your company is too small to be covered by COBRA or your company offers no worker health benefits, then you are on your own in the individual insurance market. Because it's employer-sponsored group health insurance, COBRA coverage is usually more generous than individual plans.

The details: COBRA allows you, your spouse, and eligible children to continue your employee health insurance benefits for eighteen months after you leave your job. You are guaranteed the coverage regardless of preexisting conditions and with no waiting periods. If you qualify for Medicare when you leave your job but your spouse does not, he or she can continue coverage with your employee health insurance for up to thirty-six months. You spouse is also eligible for thirty-six months of coverage if you die or divorce. You and your spouse are eligible for COBRA even if you have been laid off or fired for any reason other than gross misconduct. There are two hitches to enrolling: you must apply within sixty days and you cannot combine COBRA with any other comprehensive health insurance. One great thing about COBRA is that you are guaranteed the coverage, just as though you were working, in any state that is within your plan's coverage area, not just the state in which you were employed. If you are in an employer-sponsored HMO, however, that coverage area might be quite limited. If you plan to move and your HMO doesn't offer coverage in your new area, you should consider switching to a traditional fee-for-service or PPO plan during your company's open-enrollment period, if possible. Otherwise, you could wind up with a COBRA policy that covers only emergency services, forcing you to travel to your previous area for medical care, including regular checkups, doctor visits, and surgery.

The problem with COBRA is that it's expensive; family coverage can run well over $1,000 a month. The reason is that your company is no longer picking up part of the tab; in fact, you can be charged an extra 2 percent on the full premium (what your employer paid plus what you contributed) as an administrative fee.

Because employers must cover all employees, regardless of their health, the group usually includes a mix of risk levels. People with no health problems may find it cheaper to go for individual insurance, particularly an HSA-linked policy.

Even after your COBRA coverage period expires, it offers you a path to securing guaranteed insurance until you become eligible for Medicare. That's because once you exhaust COBRA, you fall under another federal law: HIPAA, or the Health Insurance Portability and Accountability Act of 1996. Generally, insurers operating in a state must offer the state's residents two HIPAA-eligible plans that are modeled on their two most popular individual nongroup policies. HIPAA does not, however, regulate rates; the plans are expensive since insurers must accept all qualified applicants, regardless of their health. But, like COBRA, you are guaranteed the coverage regardless of preexisting conditions and with no waiting periods. Important: You must apply for HIPAA coverage within sixty-three days of exhausting COBRA coverage or you lose the right to do so.

COBRA and HIPAA can be your route to uninterrupted, albeit expensive, comprehensive coverage until you are eligible for Medicare, especially if you or someone in your family has health problems that may be a barrier to an individual policy.

Two Other After-Work Options

If neither COBRA nor individual coverage works for you, there are two other options you should consider: short-term insurance and coverage through an association.

Short-term insurance is just what its name implies: coverage for a defined period, usually less than a year. The insurance is less expensive, the application process is simpler, and the coverage is not as difficult to qualify for as traditional insurance. However—and this is a big however—it commonly does not cover preexisting conditions. Most policies also do not cover preventive care, physicals, or immunizations. Short-term insurance is designed primarily to protect against an accident or an unexpected illness. Warning: Do not buy a short-term insurance plan if you are coming off COBRA coverage and expect to switch to HIPAA guaranteed-issue coverage within the sixty-three days in which you are allowed to do so. Buying short-term insurance can make you ineligible for the HIPAA coverage.

Another possible route to health insurance is to join a group. Several trade, fraternal, or professional organizations, many with lax membership rules, offer health insurance to their members. Preexisting conditions remain an issue. There may, however, be a relatively small price advantage.

The Last Option: Into the High-Risk Pool

If you aren't eligible for COBRA or HIPAA coverage and you can't qualify for individual insurance because of preexisting conditions, your only choice may be a high-risk pool—if your state has one. In such cases, states contract with insurers to fund a pool for normally uninsurable people. Unfortunately, the premiums are usually very high and there can be waiting lists or outright moratoriums on accepting new participants. In some states the high-risk pool is the HIPAA option for those coming off COBRA coverage, and in those cases you can't be turned down.

According to data from the Kaiser Family Foundation, as of 2006 thirty-four states had high-risk pools or some equivalent. Guaranteed-issue states don't need high-risk pools, of course. The eleven states that don't insure coverage for high-risk individuals are Arizona, Delaware, Georgia, Hawaii, Michigan, Nevada, North Carolina, Ohio, Pennsylvania, Rhode Island, and Virginia. Figure 5 groups the states based on the options for high-risk individuals.

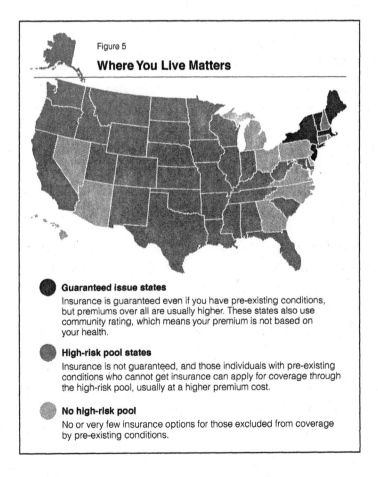

Figure 5

Where You Live Matters

Guaranteed issue states
Insurance is guaranteed even if you have pre-existing conditions, but premiums over all are usually higher. These states also use community rating, which means your premium is not based on your health.

High-risk pool states
Insurance is not guaranteed, and those individuals with pre-existing conditions who cannot get insurance can apply for coverage through the high-risk pool, usually at a higher premium cost.

No high-risk pool
No or very few insurance options for those excluded from coverage by pre-existing conditions.

States with high-risk pools, however, can have waiting periods as long as a year before preexisting conditions are covered. These waiting periods can sometimes be reduced if you have had prior coverage. The Web site of Affinity Group Underwriters (www.agu.net) has some of the best and most current information on high-risk pools in the states that offer them. From the home page, click on "Industry Links." Then scroll down to "HIPAA Related Links" and click on "State Risk Pools." There you will find direct links to each state's high-risk pool Web site if the state maintains one.

Finally, if you can't get insurance of any kind in your state you should consider moving. The fastest way to deplete your retirement nest egg is through health costs. Almost half the bankruptcies in the United States stem from overwhelming medical bills.

When All Else Fails

If, despite your planning, you are faced with significant medical bills because you are uninsured or underinsured for a procedure, you should try to bargain hard with the hospital and other providers to get a discount. According to the journal *Health Affairs*, the uninsured are billed at an average rate 2.5 times more than a health insurer would pay on behalf of a policyholder for the same service. Many hospitals are often willing to negotiate a lower price and even work out a payment arrangement. According to a 2005 survey by *USA Today*, the Kaiser Family Foundation, and the Harvard School of Public Health, 58 percent of those who tried to negotiate reported they got a lower price. This can help protect your retirement savings from being eaten up by health costs.

Unfortunately, Medicaid, which covers medical expenses for the poor, really isn't a viable option for retirees regardless of their annual income levels. The Kaiser Family Foundation points out that in most states nonparent adults are ineligible for Medicaid—even if they have *no* income at all—unless they are severely disabled. Even if you qualify, you will face a maze of regulations, limitations, and cutbacks. Many doctors refuse to accept Medicaid patients because the reimbursement rates are so low. Better to delay retirement if Medicaid appears to be your only option. Even if you've been forced to retire because of a merger or downsizing, you're unlikely to qualify.

PREPARING FOR MEDICARE

Despite concerns about its financial underpinnings, the government's Medicare program is extremely popular and will likely be around for a long time. Every retirement plan should be based on a full understanding of and preparation for the transition to Medicare. Medicare provides health insurance for:

- People sixty-five years old or older.
- People under age sixty-five who have been receiving Social Security Disability Insurance for more than two years.
- People under age sixty-five who have permanent kidney failure requiring continuing dialysis or a kidney transplant.
- People under age sixty-five diagnosed with amyotrophic lateral sclerosis, commonly known as Lou Gehrig's disease.

Medicare consists of three main programs:

- **Part A,** which covers hospital bills. You cannot opt out and are automatically enrolled in Part A when you turn sixty-five. If you have worked in the United States for at least ten years, you pay no monthly premiums for Part A; you "prepaid" for the coverage through the Medicare taxes deducted from your payroll check.
- **Part B,** which covers doctor bills and outpatient services. When you turn sixty-five, you must decide whether to enroll in Part B; most people do. For 2007, the Part B premium, which rises every year, was set at $93.50 per month for individuals with annual incomes of less than $80,000 ($160,000 for a couple). That monthly charge in-

creases to $105.80 for those making $80,000 to $100,000 a year ($160,000 to $200,000 for a couple); $124.40 for an income of $100,000 to $150,000 ($200,000 to $300,000 for a couple); $142.90 for $150,000 to $200,000 ($300,000 to $400,000 for a couple); and $161.40 for someone earning more than $200,000 ($400,000 for a couple).

- **Part D,** which covers prescription drugs. This program is voluntary.

While these three programs may seem to cover everything you'll need, there are tremendous gaps in coverage, as seen in figure 6. For instance, if you enroll in the traditional fee-for-service Medicare program, which allows you to use virtually any doctor or hospital you choose, you will almost certainly need a supplemental policy. Your supplemental policy should cover some or all of a deductible of $992

Figure 6

Some Medicare Gaps, 2007

Part A: Hospitalization	**You owe up to:**
Deductible for first 60 days in the hospital	$ 992
A second stay of 60 days or less within a year, but in a new benefit period	1,984
A third stay of 60 days or less within a year, but in a new benefit period	2,976
Coinsurance for hospital days 61 through 90	$248 a day
Coinsurance for hospital days after the 90th	$496 a day
Doing the math:	
Hospital charges for a 90-day stay	$ 8,432
Hospital charges for a 120-day stay	23,312

Part B: Doctors and outpatient services	
Premium at $93.50 per month*	$ 1,122
Deductible, annual	131
Coinsurance	20% of charges

*Higher if income exceeds $80,000

for the first sixty days you are in the hospital; coinsurance, the amount you must pay after the deductible is met, of $248 a day for hospitalization for days 61 through 90 and $496 a day for stays beyond day 90 of a benefit period; an annual deductible of $131 for Medicare Part B; and a 20 percent coinsurance payment for physician and most outpatient services received through Part B. There are also charges of more than $124 a day for days 21 through 100 in a skilled nursing facility, and charges for blood if you need a transfusion.

Two Web sites are helpful in explaining Medicare charges in detail. The first, Medicare.gov, is run by the Centers for Medicare and Medicaid Services (toll-free, 1-800-MEDICARE). The second, MedicareRights.org (toll-free, 1-800-333-4114), is run by the nonprofit Medicare Rights Center, which is based in New York City and, among other things, helps people with Medicare problems and questions.

To fill the gaps in Medicare, most people either enroll in a private Medicare HMO or PPO plan in their area under the Medicare Advantage program (which pays private insurers for each Medicare recipient they insure) or purchase a Medigap policy. You cannot combine a Medigap policy with the Medicare Advantage program. The choice between Medicare Advantage and a Medigap policy comes down to how comfortable you are with managed care and using only doctors or hospitals in a certain network.

Medicare Advantage

If you enroll in a private Medicare Advantage plan, you may have to pay an extra premium, on top of the Medicare Part B premium, to the insurer. This extra monthly premium buys you coverage for many of the extra charges you would be responsible for paying out of pocket under traditional Medicare. According to the federal Centers for Medicare and Medicaid Services, Medicare Advantage plans result in average beneficiary savings of $86 a month. However, under these private plans you are limited to certain doctors, hospitals, and—in the case of HMOs and PPOs—certain geographic service areas.

Premiums vary widely across the country. At Medicare.gov you can find all the plans and their prices for your state or area. In Kansas, where I live, there are 34 plans available; there are 151 in New York and 139 in California. Prices in all three states run from zero (which means the insurer accepts the allowance paid by Medicare as your full premium to cover you) to slightly over $200 a month, depending on the coverage. Prices are always quoted per person; family coverage is not available. Medicare Advantage rates are community-rated, meaning they are the same regardless of your health status or age. About 19 percent of Medicare recipients are enrolled in Medicare Advantage plans.

Medicare Advantage currently offers lower premiums compared to traditional Medicare plus a Medigap policy. However, co-payments and coinsurance are increasing for these plans. The private plans also cost taxpayers more than Medicare, so Congress is likely to slash spending on them, thus reducing benefits or increasing costs, before any other part of the program. If you get a serious illness, Medicare Advantage also has gaps of its own: there can be restrictions on access to some treatments.

Geography can be a bigger problem than you might expect. Diane Archer, the founder of the Medicare Rights Center, cites problems with continuity of care and service-area limits. If you travel frequently, you probably do not want to be restricted to a Medicare Advantage plan's service area. This can also be a problem if you become ill and need to live with a relative outside your service area.

"Older and disabled people often sign up for these Medicare HMOs and other Medicare Advantage plans to save money, which they will—as long as they're relatively healthy and stay in-network," Archer said. "But if they get a serious illness, they may find that certain co-pays are astronomical. People like traditional Medicare because it doesn't punish the sick."

For this reason, Archer recommends passing up Medicare Advantage and choosing traditional Medicare plus a Medigap policy—that is, if you can afford it.

Medigap Policies

The government has made it fairly easy to buy Medigap insurance to supplement traditional Medicare Part A and Part B. There are twelve standardized policies, A through L (plans H, I, and J are no longer available for new enrollment). This standardization, according to Robert Hayes of the Medicare Rights Center, has led to a "reasonably good level of customer satisfaction with Medigap policies."

When shopping for a plan, therefore, the difference you need to look for is price, which is not regulated; the benefits provided by insurers will be identical for each standardized plan. While premiums will rise with inflation in the cost of medical services, you cannot be singled out for a rate increase based on your medical condition.

Figure 7 shows the main benefits of the various Medigap plans. Note that the least expensive, but also least comprehensive, A, does not cover the $992 deductible for your first sixty days of hospitalization. Remember, too, that you could be hit with this deductible two or three times in a single calendar year. If you are on a limited income, consider paying a little extra for plan B instead. Plans K and L are low-cost alternatives to plans A through J but have fewer benefits. Instead of receiving 100 percent coverage, you receive 50 percent (plan K) or 75 percent (plan L) for some of the most common Part B charges. The most popular plans, C and F, are among the most comprehensive.

At Medicare.gov you can find prices for Medigap policies. For plan F, monthly premiums in Kansas range from $82 to $240; in New York, $142 to $344; and in California, $102 to $374.

Once you sign up for Medicare Part B, you have six months to purchase a Medigap policy without concerns about preexisting conditions. After six months you can be denied coverage for preexisting conditions or denied coverage altogether.

If you like to travel internationally, you should select a Medigap policy that will pay for emergency care outside the United States.

Figure 7

Medigap Plans, 2007

	— Plans —								
Gaps in Medicare Part A	**A**	**B**	**C**	**D**	**E**	**F**	**G**	**K**	**L**
Hospital deductible *Covers $992 in each benefit period*		●	●	●	●	●	●	50%*	75%*
Hospital coinsurance *Days 61-90 ($248) and days 91-150 ($496) in hospital*	●	●	●	●	●	●	●	●	●
First three pints of blood		●	●	●	●	●	●	50%*	75%*
Emergency care outside the United States *80% of costs during the first 60 days of each trip, after an annual deductible of $250, up to a maximum lifetime benefit of $50,000*			●	●	●	●	●		
Gaps in Medicare Part B									
Annual deductible *Covers $131*			●			●			
Services coinsurance *Includes doctors' services, laboratory and X-ray services, durable medical equipment, and hospital outpatient services*	●	●	●	●	●	●	●	50%*	75%*

— continued —

Figure 7

Medigap Plans, 2007 *continued*

Gaps in Medicare Part B	— Plans —								
	A	B	C	D	E	F	G	K	L
Excess charges benefits *Under federal law, the excess limit is 15% more than Medicare's approved charge when the provider does not accept Medicare assignment (under New York law, it is 5% for most services)*						100%	80%		
Preventive medical care *Up to $120 per year for non-Medicare-covered physicals, preventive tests, and services*					●				
Preventive medical care *100% of coinsurance for Part B-covered preventive care services, after the Part B deductible has been paid*	●	●	●	●	●	●	●	50%*	75%*
Skilled nursing facility daily coinsurance *Covers $124 per day for days 21-100 in each benefit period.*			●	●	●	●	●		
At-home recovery benefit *Up to $40 each visit for custodial care after an illness, injury or surgery, maximum benefit of $1,600 a year.*				●			●		

*Out of pocket maximums
Pays 100% of Part A and Part B coinsurance after annual maximum has been spent

Plan K: $4,140   **Plan L:** $2,070

Source: Medicare Rights Center

RX FOR YOUR WALLET

Gone are the days when most people with drug coverage paid a flat co-pay of $1, $3, or $5 for a prescription. Co-payments are rising dramatically or being replaced with coinsurance, in which patients pay a percentage of a drug's cost instead of a flat per-prescription amount. That coinsurance, especially for brand-name drugs, can be 20 percent, 50 percent, or more as insurers shift the costs to consumers. Plus, drug prices are increasing at a pace more than double the overall inflation rate, and more and more medical conditions are being treated primarily through prescription drugs. It pays to understand how to get affordable prescriptions whether you're retiring early or relying on Medicare for your coverage

Comparing Prices

One of the most effective methods for lowering the cost of prescription drugs is to shop around. When comparing prices on your prescriptions, first check to see if your brand-name drug has one or more generic equivalents. Often your doctor will prescribe the brand-name drug; ask him or her to indicate on the prescription that a generic equivalent can be substituted.

Usually big drug chains offer the best retail prices simply because of their huge volume of business. Among the chains, Costco's pharmacies often have lower prices, especially for generic drugs. Costco charges an annual membership fee to shop at its stores, but not for use of the pharmacy.

Let's compare some prices on some popular brand-name and generic drugs. Figure 8 gives the retail prices for five top-selling brand-name drugs at Costco (www.costco.com); CVS (www.cvs.com); Drugstore.com (www.drugstore.com), an online pharmacy; Walgreens (www.walgreens.com); and Wal-Mart (www.walmart.com). Figure 9 shows the prices at the same concerns for five top-selling generic drugs. All prices are for a thirty-day supply of the most

Figure 8

Price-Hunting for Brand-Name Drugs

Retailer	Lipitor (20 mg) For high cholesterol	Zocor (20 mg) For high cholesterol	Prevacid (30 mg) For stomach acid	Nexium (40 mg) For stomach acid	Zoloft (50 mg) For depression
Costco	$110.54	$141.48	$139.34	$142.87	$ 84.17
CVS	127.99	154.99	159.99	156.99	95.59
Drugstore.com	109.19	139.99	141.99	136.99	87.14
Walgreen	121.99	149.99	162.99	161.99	93.99
Wal-Mart (Mail-order)	109.54	137.78	142.78	141.68	80.62

commonly prescribed strengths. By the time this book is published, many prices likely will have changed—in fact, the cost of these five brand-name drugs has gone up from 5 percent to 15 percent just since 2006. All but Wal-Mart's prices are available online; you must call Wal-Mart to get its prices. In the case of Wal-Mart, I have given

Figure 9

Price-Hunting for Generic Drugs

Retailer	Lisinopril (20 mg) For high blood pressure	Atenolol (50 mg) For heart-beat, blood pressure	Amoxicillin (250 mg) Antibiotic	Hydrochlo-rothiazide (50 mg) For high blood pressure	Furo-semide (20 mg) For high blood pressure
Costco	$ 5.00	$ 5.49	$ 8.84	$ 5.00	$ 5.69
CVS	13.69	7.99	11.09	3.90	5.68
Drugstore.com	10.99	3.66	7.99	3.90	2.70
Walgreen	14.99	3.68	11.99	8.79	2.96
Wal-Mart (Mail-order)	19.36	14.84	5.68	5.32	5.32

only its mail-order prices, which can be different from its stores prices. Store prices also vary around the country, depending on competition and other local factors. The Wal-Mart stores also offer a thirty-day supply of some generic drugs for a flat rate of $4; that deal is not available through mail order.

As these two charts make clear, it pays to shop around for your prescriptions. For example, the price for Lipitor ranged from a low of $109.19 at Drugstore.com to a high of $127.99 at CVS, a difference of $18.80, or $225.60 a year. Nexium ranged from $136.99 at Drugstore.com to $161.99 at Walgreens, a difference of $25, or $300 a year.

But it is the price differences for the generic drugs where things really get interesting. Lisinopril, the blood pressure drug, came in for a low of $5 at Costco and a high of $19.36 Wal-Mart (mail order), a more than threefold difference. That adds up to $172.32 a year. Atenolol, prescribed to regulate heartbeat and control blood pressure, ran from $3.66 at Drugstore.com to $14.84 at Wal-Mart (mail order), a difference of $11.18, or $134.16 a year. Considering that many of us seem to need an entire diet of prescription drugs as we get older, these savings can easily total $500 to $1,000 a year.

You should consider shipping charges when comparing prices of your drugs. Such charges, however, are usually relatively modest and are not pegged to order size. So if you have several prescriptions to fill, shipping costs will be a very small additional charge on top of each drug's price. Some companies advertise a flat rate for shipping, or even free shipping, but check first because there can be exceptions.

If you don't have access to the Internet, here are the phone numbers for the companies discussed, although the numbers are subject to change:

Costco	1-800-955-2292
CVS	1-888-607-4287
Drugstore.com	1-800-378-4786
Walgreens	1-877-250-5823
Wal-Mart (mail order)	1-800-273-3455

Split Pills

When it comes to prescriptions, managing costs can seem more like a bunch of small tactical assaults than a major budget-cutting strategy. But these small costs quickly add up. It also helps to recognize that drug prices have little connection to the dosage prescribed. For example, Lipitor, the high cholesterol drug that according to the U.S. Agency for Healthcare Research and Quality is the most prescribed drug in America, has sales of more than $7 billion a year. Drugstore.com sells a thirty-day supply of 20-milligram pills—the most commonly prescribed dose at one a day—for $109.19. But Lipitor is available in strengths of 10, 20, 40, and 80 milligrams, and Drugstore.com sells thirty of the weaker 10-milligram tablets for $81.89, thirty of the 40-milligram tablets for $109.19, and thirty of the 80-milligram tablets for only $111.29. You can make this Alice-in-Wonderland pricing work to your advantage.

Because many pills, not just Lipitor, cost pretty much the same regardless of the dosage, pill-splitting can be a great cost-saving tactic. For example, if your doctor prescribes 20 milligrams of Lipitor a day, you can ask for a prescription of 40-milligram tablets that can be cut in half to last twice as long—saving you 50 percent.

As it happens, some insurance companies are now urging their clients to practice pill-splitting and even offering pill-splitting devices to make the job easier. Pill-splitting works only if a pill comes in double your needed dose. Pill-cutting devices won't cut pills into thirds, and cutting pills into fourths can be tricky, altering your dosage day to day. Odd-shaped pills are more difficult; you can find more expensive devices that make cutting irregularly shaped pills like Viagra a snap. Pill-cutters range from as cheap as $3 at your local drugstore to as much as $25 online for a more versatile model. (Just put "pill-splitter" into an Internet search engine like Google to track down options or go directly to SeniorShops.com or a similar Web site.)

Capsules with powder or gel inside obviously can't be split. And some medicines, like extended-relief tablets or some migraine drugs, should not be cut because they work as their various layers dissolve. Consult your doctor to see if any or all of your prescriptions can be split.

Buying Drugs from Canada

If you need to track down even more savings, particularly on brand-name drugs, look north of the border. Drugs in Canada are cheaper because the government controls the prices. However, there are some potential pitfalls. The practice depends on the willingness of the Canadian government to allow its country to serve as a backdoor pharmacy for the United States; it also flies in the face of U.S. law and is under growing pressure from the pharmaceutical industry. Nonetheless, some states are getting in on the act, whether encouraging residents to buy cheaper drugs from Canada or importing them directly for groups such as state workers. Thanks to the Internet, you don't have to take a bus to Winnipeg to save money on your prescriptions.

How much money? A lot. Look at figure 10 for the prices of the popular drugs from Canada Pharmacy (www.canadapharmacy.com), which is based in Surrey, British Columbia, and offers only telephone and Internet service. A thirty-day supply of 20-milligram Lipitor tablets from Canada Pharmacy costs $55, nearly 50 percent less than

Figure 10

Saving on Brand-Name Drugs From Canada

	Lipitor (20 mg) For high cholesterol	Zocor (20 mg) For high cholesterol	Prevacid (30 mg) For stomach acid	Nexium (40 mg) For stomach acid	Zoloft (50 mg) For depression
Lowest U.S. price*	$109.19	$137.78	$139.34	$136.99	$80.62
Canada Pharmacy	55.00	63.00	87.00	87.74	61.50

*Lowest price of retailers surveyed in Figure 8.

the lowest U.S. price of $109.19 at Drugstore.com. If you buy drugs from Canada *and* split them, the savings are even greater. Caution: While brand-name drugs are cheaper in Canada, most generic drugs are as cheap, if not cheaper, in the United States.

I called Canada Pharmacy's toll-free number (1-800-891-0844) to find out some of the details involved in ordering drugs from Canada over the Internet. It is relatively easy. Representatives are available twenty-four hours a day, seven days a week, and the waiting time to speak with someone was far shorter than is typical in the United States. To get an account started at Canada Pharmacy you must simply fax the company a valid form of ID, such as a driver's license, passport, or birth certificate. Then you fax the prescriptions from your American doctor. The prescriptions are sent to a Canadian doctor who confirms the specifications and writes a Canadian prescription for the drugs you need. The Canadian prescription is filled and shipped via regular mail. The whole process takes two to three weeks. Refills are faster because they don't have to be routed through a Canadian doctor. The only risk is a hang-up with U.S. Customs, but a Canada Pharmacy representative said this happens "not too often," in part because prescriptions are shipped from a U.S.-based facility as well as Surrey.

Canada Pharmacy sells just about every drug available in the United States, except controlled substances like narcotics, which cannot be shipped internationally. You can check the price for a drug, in U.S. dollars, on the company's Web site. Drugs are dispensed only in quantities listed on the site, usually in packs of ninety, so it helps if your prescriptions are written that way. But if a prescription is for less than ninety days, the pharmacy will deduct the excess out of future refills.

Shipping is $10 (U.S.) per order, regardless of the number of items. Customers can opt to pay a onetime shipping charge of $50 (U.S.) and get lifetime shipping for everyone listed on the account. You can pay for your prescriptions by credit card, electronic check, or money order.

Medicare Part D

When you turn sixty-five, Medicare can kick in to help with your prescription costs—if you sign up. Medicare Part D, the prescription coverage plan for Medicare beneficiaries, went into effect at the beginning of 2006. Because many insurance companies offer so many permutations of the coverage, it can be extremely confusing. In many states there are scores of plans available with different formularies, or lists of drugs that are covered, as well as varying co-pays and deductibles. You must be careful that the drugs you take are on the formulary of the plan you sign up for.

Under Part D, insurance companies have wide latitude to vary both co-pays and annual deductibles, although no plan can have a deductible higher than $265. Premiums are all over the place. According to Medicare.gov, Kansas has sixty-three plans with premiums running from $11.30 to $102.30 a month; New York has sixty-one plans, from $9.50 to $82.10; and California has fifty-three plans, from $9.70 to $80.90. According to the Medicare Rights Center, the average monthly premium in 2007 was $27.35.

For those with retiree health benefits that include prescription coverage from their former employers, there is a special danger. If you decide to try Medicare Part D instead of your retiree drug coverage, you may lose all of your retiree medical benefits. In other words, stay put—or lose everything. That's because some companies say they can't separate drug coverage from a package of health benefits. (There are some companies, of course, that have no trouble separating the coverage; they unceremoniously dump retirees from drug coverage when they hit sixty-five, suggesting they sign up for Medicare Part D.)

Part D also has gaps in coverage. In a Medicare Advantage HMO or PPO, Part D may require an extra premium. There is the annual deductible of up to $265 as well as co-payments, depending on the plan. Then there is the infamous "doughnut hole." If your cumulative drug expenses in a year reach $2,400 (for 2007), you're suddenly on your own. The drug benefit disappears until your costs hit $5,451.25—potentially leaving you on the hook for $3,051.25. Some big insurers are able to offer coverage for the doughnut hole in their most expensive policies because they can negotiate such good prices with drug makers that they don't end up spending any more money, which they are not allowed to do, to cover this gap. According to government and other estimates, Part D is expected to save, on average, only 37 percent of out-of-pocket drug costs.

Despite the gaps, if you turn sixty-five and are not covered by a retiree health plan that includes prescription drug benefits or if you get kicked out of your retiree plan, you probably should sign up for Part D even if you don't currently take a lot of prescriptions. AARP found that many people will pay less enrolled in Part D than if they skipped the coverage and bought their drugs exclusively from Canada. Generally, you can switch plans during an annual open enrollment period that runs from November 15 to December 31.

Help from the Drug Companies

If you don't have prescription drug coverage, you may be eligible for free drugs from pharmaceutical companies. Virtually all the drug makers will provide free medicines for those who have no drug coverage and whose incomes fall below certain levels. The income limits are not always that strict—in some cases people earning as much as $60,000 a year can qualify. One unavoidable wrinkle is that you must apply separately to each company that makes your medications. The drugs are commonly dispensed through doctors, and patients usually have to requalify regularly.

You can check the Web sites of companies that manufacture your prescribed drugs or the Web site of the Pharmaceutical Research and Manufacturers of America (www.phrma.org) to find out more about these programs, which are lumped together under what the trade group calls the Partnership for Prescription Assistance. If you don't have access to the Internet, you can call the Partnership for Prescription Assistance at 1-888-477-2669.

Juggling the Pharmacies

Whether or not private insurance or Medicare Part D covers you, if you shop for prescription drugs solely on the basis of price you will most likely get different prescriptions filled by different pharmacies. That can be fine if you are certain you understand the side effects of drugs you are taking and how they interact with other drugs; if you are not sure about interactions or need help sorting it out, you may need another solution. The advantage of buying all your prescriptions from one pharmacy is that a pharmacist is able, often with the help of a computer program, to keep track of what you are taking and warn you of conflicts and problems.

One option for those with *no* drug coverage is to get generic drugs from a single U.S. pharmacy that offers competitive, low prices for them and to order your brand-name drugs from Canada. Explain to the pharmacist exactly what you are doing, give him or her a list of your brand-name drugs, and ask for help spotting any unfavorable interactions. Since the pharmacy's profit markup on generics is much greater than it is for brand-name drugs, most pharmacists will not have a problem providing the information to you. In fact, it is not an unusual request since pharmacies often have customers whose drug coverage plans require certain maintenance medicines to be purchased from distant mail-order companies or who get some of their drugs from the Veterans Administration.

LONG-TERM CARE

Virtually everyone thinks that health insurance is a necessity. But a lot of people are confused, with good reason, about whether they need long-term-care insurance.

There are several problems with this type of insurance. Deena Katz, the financial planner in Coral Gables, Florida, advocates such insurance in certain circumstances but points out that it hasn't been around that long. "Insurance companies have been in and out of these policies," she explained. "At one time there were one hundred fifty companies offering them; now there are very few. So the commitment is a little wobbly." In a March 2007 article the *New Yo Times* cited unnecessary delays and bureaucracies in the claim-filing process for long-term care; in California alone, nearly one in four claims were denied in 2005.

In addition, long-term-care insurance is getting more expensive and covering less; worse still, the regulations governing it are inconsistent. Existing policyholders can face premium increases, especially for policies that were underpriced as insurers tried to gain market share in recent years. The AARP Web site (www.aarp.org) cites the case of an Ohio couple who saw the annual premiums on their eight-year-old policy jump to $4,862 from $3,255, a 50 percent increase. While thirty-four states have adopted or are in the process of adopting model regulations to stabilize premiums for long-term care based on recommendations by the National Association of Insurance Commissioners (NAIC), policies purchased before the regulations were passed in each state are not covered. The NAIC Web site (www.naic.org) contains links to the various state insurance departments. Some of these links are helpful, some less so. In the end, you may have to contact your state insurance department for its regulations on long-term-care insurance.

The state-by-state reforms have made a difference in the value of long-term-care policies. Foremost, there is relatively better standardization in the policies than in the past. This is especially important, Katz says, when it comes to the definitions of conditions and health events that will trigger benefit payments. Keep in mind, though, that long-term-care is not age-specific: you don't have to be old and in a nursing home for it to kick in. Mary Lou Odle, a Kansas State University extension agent in Salina, Kansas, often helps people who are trying to understand long-term-care insurance. "Long-term policies vary," she said. "In addition to nursing home care, they may cover home health care, assisted living, and adult day care."

Katz said: "Long-term-care insurance is hard to understand, it varies with every state, and it is not the panacea we would like it to be. On the other hand, there are good uses for it. The reasons people should buy long-term care are for asset protection, estate preservation, and what I call the fear factor: if someone lives far away from family members and there is no one to take care of them, it is certainly a lot easier to go into a long-term-care facility as a paying patient than to have to go broke and accept Medicaid. The insurance is expensive, but you may be willing to accept a lesser quality of life today—in other words, bear the cost of buying the insurance—for the promise of tomorrow. The younger you are when you buy long-term-care insurance, of course, the less the premiums are."

Most experts agree that the two groups of people who should not purchase long-term-care insurance are those with high assets—enough money to afford care on their own—and those with low assets—too little money to worry about protecting it. The latter group should just count on Medicaid taking over after they have exhausted their resources. (The only problem: in many states, relying on Medicaid can adversely affect the assets of the spouse who doesn't need long-term care. You should seek advice on this topic from a lawyer or your county or state agency for the aging.)

The real conundrum, of course, is figuring out how high or low your assets must be to opt out of long-term-care. Katz set $200,000 as the asset level, including the equity in your home, below which you probably should not buy long-term-care insurance. But, she concedes, "there are disagreements about this all the time," and "some advisers say one hundred thousand dollars." Those with higher levels of assets just have to make decisions based on their cash flow and what they feel they can afford. According to *USA Today,* the average nursing home stay runs about $5,000 a month, and Katz notes that the average stay is about ninety days, which would cost $15,000. "Those who stay longer than that stay about three years," she said. "At the tail end of those statistics are people who are in nursing homes for many years."

What about those whose assets fall in the middle range? If you are single, aren't concerned about leaving an estate, or do not live far away from people who can help you, you may not need long-term-care insurance. Katz advises that you should also review your family medical background when making a decision. For instance, if a long-term, incapacitating illness, such as Alzheimer's disease or rheumatoid arthritis, runs in your family, the prospect of paying for years living in a nursing home might nudge you to buy a long-term-care policy if your budget allows it.

You need to decide how long you can pay for long-term care on your own, Katz explained, adding that long-term care should be viewed as strictly catastrophic coverage. "If you can afford a short stay in a nursing home for a broken hip, you don't need the insurance for that," she said. "You want it for a five-year stay because you have Alzheimer's."

Katz warned that many people don't investigate the odds and the averages and don't really know how to buy long-term-care insurance. "Too many people are 'sold' this insurance," she contended. She urges her clients to buy only as much insurance as they need. "You may not need insurance to cover all your costs, or you may not be able to afford full coverage," she said. "Whatever you can afford to buy is going to defray some of the expense. If a nursing home is charging $150 a day and you have a $60-a-day policy, that's $60 a day you don't have to spend." Katz also cautions against the pitch from many insurance companies that you need lifetime coverage. Katz says you really only need four to five years of coverage. The three-year average for longer nursing home stays reflects the average life expectancy for people with serious, long-term illnesses.

Not surprisingly, Katz recommends consulting with a financial planner about long-term-care insurance. For instance, some states offer tax incentives for buying long-term-care insurance. You should also check with your employer's benefits department; long-term-care insurance is sometimes offered through employers at much more favorable rates.

Even if you decide that long-term-care insurance is for you, you can be turned down for health reasons if you have preexisting medical conditions. "This is a big issue," Katz said, "and another reason other than price for getting these policies earlier. You're less likely to have health problems at fifty than at seventy."

If a company turns you down for long-term-care insurance, don't despair. Try another. That's the lesson Mary H. "Jody" Parsons of Manhattan, Kansas, learned when she set out to buy the insurance after her husband died in March 2005, when she was seventy-three. One company, which required a physical exam, turned her down twice because of a relatively minor case of osteoarthritis in her right knee. But she applied to another company and was accepted based simply on her medical records and a telephone interview. She bought a policy that will pay $70 a day for up to two years, or a bit over $51,000. Her premium is $111.16 a month, or $1,333.92 a year.

"Who knows if I'll need this or not," Parsons said. "It's a crap-shoot, but I think it's worth the gamble. I mainly wanted to protect my estate. I don't want to have to spend all my money on health care. I thought about buying life insurance instead, but that would have been too expensive."

7

Key No. 3: Your Unexpected Assets

Follow your bliss.
—JOSEPH CAMPBELL

If you've been whipsawed by the stock market or seen the value of your house head south, you could be forgiven for looking askance at your retirement plans. If you're already retired, you might be worried about staying that way without looking for a soup kitchen.

Well, try to relax and remember one of the central points of this book: *you can increase your income by cutting expenses.* You can do this without becoming a cheapskate. You don't have to reuse tea bags or make guitar picks out of expired credit cards. The goal is to be economical, not cheap—to maximize the power of your money. This can lead, especially in retirement, to the simpler, less stressful life that many baby boomers say they seek.

In chapter 3 we looked at various concrete ways to cut back and simplify your life in order to boost income. Chapter 9 contains a worksheet for calculating your net worth: basically adding up your assets (what you own) and liabilities (what you owe) and subtracting the latter from the former. There's also a handy consumer Web site (www.practicalmoneyskills.com) that can help you with this and much more. For purposes of comparison, according to the Federal Reserve families in the United States with a head of household who is fifty-five to sixty-four had a median net worth in 2004 (the latest year available) of $248,700; the average was $843,800. The median (half above, half below) is a more meaningful figure since a relatively few very rich people can inflate the average.

CONSIDER ALL YOUR ASSETS

As you make plans, it's important to keep in mind that *you,* and your ability to reduce expenses, are an asset. In addition to your cost-cutting skills, there's another aspect of you—which we'll look at later in this chapter—that can sometimes lead to a fatter bank account: your unrealized dreams. It's impossible, of course, to give dollar amounts to dreams or list them on your net worth worksheet. But they should not be undervalued or overlooked in your planning.

One trick to saving money, as we discussed in chapter 3, is to think small. *Sweat the small stuff*. Overlooking little things in your budget, like that $1 can of soda, can be a big mistake. It's also important that you actually save the money and not fritter it away on another little thing. Keep track of what you save. Open a bank savings account solely for your weekly savings on little things; each month, shift the money into a higher-yielding account like a mutual fund.

Stacia Ragolia, the author of *The Frugal Woman's Guide to a Rich Life* (Thomas Nelson, 2003), told me once in an interview that people often think too big when it comes to savings. "They think they can't save money unless they save ten thousand dollars at a time," she said. "But one or two hundred dollars a week [from cutting expenses] . . . can easily grow to ten thousand dollars in a year or so. She also suggested putting some of the money you save into an emergency fund so you don't have to reach for plastic when something unexpected happens. "When you have money saved up, you can avoid going into debt for an emergency. That's the way a lot of people end up in debt and in trouble. They have a health emergency or a house problem; if they have no financial buffer, suddenly they're in debt."

Your talent for cutting expenses and still living well is limited only by your imagination. It's an asset you can develop.

My wife and I used to buy commercial cleaning products for our home that were very specialized: one thing for tile, another for windows. To save money, we started using vinegar mixed with water for just about every cleaning job—at a fraction of the cost. Vinegar mixed with water cleans well and doesn't contain the toxic chemicals found in many commercial cleaners.

Food, dining out, and related expenses can be a big source of excessive or impulse spending. Poor planning is often at fault. Most of the time when my wife and I have ordered a $20 pizza delivered to our house or gone to a mediocre neighborhood restaurant and dropped $30 to $50 for dinner, it has been because we have neglected shopping and have nothing at home appealing to eat, or we were tired and didn't feel like cooking. A little planning—keeping enough food in the house and storing some prepared easy-to-fix meals in the freezer—can help eliminate this kind of spending. It might also increase happiness, since we are rarely satisfied—either with the food or with the financial outlay—after one of these spur-of-the-moment restaurant meals. It's better value for your money to dine out when you're doing so for its own sake at a place you really like rather than as a panic reaction to being out of groceries or tired.

If you go to the movies several times a month at $5 to $12 a ticket and drop $5 or $10 on overpriced popcorn and junk food, consider joining a DVD service like Netflix, which allows a number of movies each month for a flat rate. Buy a popcorn popper and watch the savings grow.

Your retirement plans may well include turning some noncash assets into money. This means selling things you don't need: those extra cars or some furniture that may not fit in a smaller house. If you can't get a fair price, donate the items to charity and take a tax deduction. First, of course, check with the Internal Revenue Service or a tax adviser for the rules on such deductions.

Depending on where you live, it might be a smart idea to hold a yard sale. This can be a great way to clear out a lot of things you might not want to carry into the next, less expensive, phase of your life. Depending on what you're selling, you might be surprised at the money you take in. In the early 1980s, my wife and I were moving from a house in Houston to a small apartment in New York City. We held a Saturday yard sale. We advertised in the classifieds and put up posters in the neighborhood and notices on bulletin boards in local grocery stores, health clubs, and community centers. The sale was scheduled to start at 9 A.M., but at 6 we had antique and used furniture dealers ringing our doorbell. They wanted to see what we had before it was picked over. The day was sunny and mild, and we had a steady stream of buyers. Our total take was a bit over $3,000.

Because we weren't thinking much about retirement in those days, we spent the money. But had we invested it at 6.5 percent, it would have grown to almost $15,000 by now. If we had invested it at 6.5 percent and added just $100 a month, it would now be worth about $87,000. Had we put it in a mutual fund that took advantage of the stock boom of the 1990s—let's assume 12 percent growth—and added the same $100 a month, that $3,000 would today be worth more than $220,000.

I don't even remember how we spent the $3,000. Talk about missed opportunities!

Family Matters

If you stand to inherit money, the asset value of your family is obvious. I would, however, like to look at family assets from a somewhat different perspective.

As we grow older, having family members who can help with the chores of daily living can prove to be a hidden asset that can delay, lessen, or make unnecessary the expense of caregivers or assisted living arrangements. In addition, as we saw in chapter 6, the presence of caring family members could be one factor in allowing you to dodge the cost of long-term-care insurance. The savings could amount to $1,000 a year or more.

This has certainly been the case with my family. My father, who died in 1999, was able to live in his own home the last few years of his life despite serious illnesses. My mother cared for him, with help from other family members. My mother, in turn, who is now in her late eighties, has been able to continue living in her home despite serious vision problems because my sisters and brothers live nearby. They take turns taking her shopping and to medical appointments. I know not all of us can count on that level of family support, especially given our mobile society and the degree to which we are scattered. But when it is available it is a valuable asset not to be overlooked. It is one reason that people who retire far from family—like the Ensmingers in chapter 4—sometimes move back home as they get older and need assistance.

If you will be drawing on your family for this sort of help in retirement, you *should* try to think of it in financial terms—not simply in order to budget for yourself, but also to head off a fight over your estate that can wind up benefiting lawyers as much as your heirs. Some sensible precautions can save a lot of money and grief down the line. It can also relieve a relative's occasional feelings of burden for helping out, making the arrangements far more practical in the short run, too.

As you talk to family members about how they may be able to pitch in if you become ill, keep in mind that they may not realize how emotional things might get in the future. Les Kotzer, an estate lawyer in Toronto, Canada, says that most estate fights are not just over money. "They're also over memories," he said. "These memories can create such bitter warfare that family members will sometimes spend more money on legal fees than the assets in question are worth." He recalls two clients—brothers—who fought in his office over a Howdy Doody lunch box in their father's estate. "One brother said, 'That lunch box has the smell of my childhood on it, and I'm not giving it to my brother,'" Kotzer said. The other brother finally relented, but the two parted on unfriendly terms. In another case, two brothers got into a fight in Kotzer's office over a sports trophy that belonged to their father. One brother threw a heavy law book at the other, barely missing his head. Kotzer sent them to another lawyer.

Cases like these prompted Kotzer and his law partner, Barry Fish, to write *The Family Fight: Planning to Avoid It* (Continental Atlantic Publications, 2002). The book offers commonsense, plainly written advice that is applicable in both Canada and the United States. It is sometimes hard to find in bookstores, but it can be ordered from Internet booksellers like Amazon.com or from Kotzer's Web site (www.familyfight.com). The book can also be ordered toll-free at 1-877-439-3999.

For Kotzer, planning is vital to help families sidestep expenses and acrimony. For instance, if someone needs help as he or she grows older, how does this responsibility—and possible expense—get divided among family members? "Death is not the only issue that can lead to family fights," Kotzer said. "Someone's incapacity can also start a family war. People need to plan for both with a will and a durable power of attorney."

Kotzer also advises parents to meet with their children to work out solutions in advance. "I've never had a parent come to me and say, 'I want my kids to fight.' Yet the children end up in fights because the parents have done no planning or have planned poorly. They've had no discussions with their children or have made some very bad assumptions." One of those assumptions, he added, is that children will exercise goodwill and settle things amicably. Another is that everything will be fine if each child receives an equal share in an estate.

"Parents should never assume goodwill among their children if there have been no prior agreements or discussions," he said. "They should never make one sibling dependent on the goodwill of another sibling. Then it's often the lawyers who have to work it out. And once you get lawyers involved, the relationship between siblings is never the same."

The idea that equal shares are fair may not be fair at all, he continued. "If one child has been a caregiver for years, would he or she be satisfied with an equal share? Or what if parents have given a lot more money along the way to one child than another? Are equal shares fair then?"

Kotzer cited the case of a woman who had taken care of her mother for years and had planned to live in the mother's home after her death. But the mother left the house equally to the woman and her brother. The brother wanted the money, so he went to court and forced a sale. In the end, his sister was forced out of a house that her mother told her would always be hers.

When wishes aren't spelled out, problems can arise from second marriages, too. "There can be two sets of heirs with nothing in common," Kotzer said. "They may actually hate each other."

One of his clients, whose father had remarried, was from a wealthy family. "When the father died," Kotzer recalled, he left everything to his second wife with the understanding that she would leave everything to his son when she died. But instead, she left everything to her two children, and my client got nothing. His stepsiblings won't even let him see his family pictures, which are now theirs."

Kotzer urges people to have their financial records organized to avoid surprises and family fights. "You can leave a good will but still leave a mess if things are disorganized," he said. "Keep good records so that your children aren't so vulnerable to fighting at a difficult time."

He also warns against do-it-yourself will kits, citing the case of a woman who prepared her own will, leaving her "personal moneys" to her two sisters and everything else to her husband. It turned out that she had some money in checking and savings accounts, plus hundreds of thousands of dollars in certificates of deposit. The husband and the woman's sisters fought over what "personal moneys" meant: the sisters asserted that they included the CDs, while the husband said they were only the small amounts. A judge ruled in favor of the husband, but only after hard feelings had developed and a lot of money had been spent on lawyers—far more money than the woman had saved with the do-it-yourself kit.

"I tell people that the most important assets they have are not in their banks or safety deposit boxes but in the family photo album—in the faces of their children and loved ones in that album," Kotzer said.

Don't Overlook Social Security

When you're trying to balance your assets and liabilities against your needs when you retire, you also should not forget Social Security—or sell it short. Although chapter 8 looks at Social Security in greater detail, I think it's important to view it as an asset that you will have access to when you are sixty-two. The longer you wait to collect it, the more you get. But, presumably, if you are trying to figure out how to retire early you are likely to tap into your Social Security benefits as soon as possible.

Again, consider Joe and Sue Sample. Their combined Social Security benefits when they are sixty-two will be $26,400 a year for as long as they live. Assume for a moment that the $26,400 represents the 4 percent that a retiree can withdraw from a nest egg without depleting it. Looking at it that way, the $26,400 payout represents savings of more than $650,000. Now that's not the way Social Security works. But $650,000 does represent the amount you would need to replace the Social Security benefit of $26,400 so that the payment would not run out in your lifetime. Remember, too, that Social Security benefits increase along with the cost of living, so that theoretical "savings" of $650,000 also increases accordingly.

I know some financial planners and accountants would probably cringe at this approach because of the pay-as-you-go structure of Social Security. But you have contributed to Social Security all your working life and are entitled to the benefits. Why not view them as an asset like anything else?

Your Second Act

What about your dreams? Survey after survey shows that most people, especially the baby boomers, do not want a traditional retirement that is akin to being constantly on vacation. People want to be challenged and stimulated in this next phase of life, and that will often include working. It doesn't mean a traditional job, or even a part-time job, and all the baggage that goes with it. After all, you are planning early retirement to free yourself from wage slavery. You don't want to jump from the frying pan into the fire!

"Follow your bliss," admonished the late teacher and scholar Joseph Campbell. That's pretty good advice, especially as you contemplate your second act. What is your bliss or your passion or your interest? What turns you on? Is there a hobby you really like? Many times there is little relationship between what you do for a living and your bliss. Think of those stories you read in newspapers of grandfathers and grandmothers who have returned to college to finish their degrees or go to medical school. They are following their bliss. Grandma Moses, a farm wife, was in her seventies when she taught herself to paint. "If I didn't start painting, I would have raised chickens," she told Edward R. Murrow in a television interview. "I would never sit back in a rocking chair, waiting for someone to help."

If you're uncertain about your bliss, you probably need to embark on some self-exploration and discovery to find what you really enjoy. Try some new things. Ever think you might like to teach? There's a teacher shortage in many parts of the country, and for those with a college degree it's not hard to get a teaching certificate in most states. Don't forget the Peace Corps, which has no upper age limit and is eagerly recruiting baby boomers. Christine Torres, a public affairs specialist with the Peace Corps' Chicago regional office, stressed the importance of the boomers in a 2007 interview with the *Mid-County Journal*, a suburban St. Louis, Missouri, newspaper. "After all, this is the JFK generation, and the Peace Corps was founded under JFK in 1961," she said. "In fact, in talking with our older volunteers, JFK's call to service with the Peace Corps still resonates very strongly with them. If they couldn't join in the 1960s, they can do it now."

Sometimes the connection takes a little creativity, but often your bliss can produce an income.

I knew an electrical engineer who was an avid bicycle rider. Just before he retired, he spent three weeks at a school for bicycle mechanics. After he retired, he took a part-time job working as a repairman in a bicycle shop and also organizing local bicycle tours; he later opened his own repair shop. He's making money and following his bliss.

A French orthopedic surgeon with a lifelong passion for art retired and applied for admission to a prestigious art academy. He was accepted and today his paintings sell briskly.

A retired English professor became a broker in Navajo rugs after years of collecting them as a hobby.

Then there are several faculty members in the auto restoration program at McPherson College in McPherson, Kansas, who followed their bliss to this small town of 14,000 about an hour's drive north of Wichita. One had been an electrical engineer with NASA; another left a career in graphic design. Now they teach students to lovingly restore old cars in a program that grants the bachelor of science degree and is one of the main sources of antique car specialists in the United States.

The possibilities are truly endless and limited only by your imagination and interests. It is usually true that if you are where you want to be and doing what you want to do, things have an uncanny way of falling into place. Joseph Campbell added that if you follow your bliss, "doors will open where you would not have thought there would be doors, and where there wouldn't be a door for anyone else." He also wrote that following your bliss puts you "on a kind of track, which has been there all the while waiting for you, and the life that you ought to be living is the one you are living."

Retirement can give you the opportunity to restore harmony to your life if you follow Campbell's advice. Better, of course, to have followed it from the beginning. But we are not perfect. Retirement gives us a second chance.

Class Starts When the Phone Rings

The historian David McCullough has said that most people have in their homes one of the most amazing research and learning devices ever invented: the lowly telephone. If you don't know something, he says, call someone who does. Alexander Graham Bell's invention has some other virtues that McCullough didn't mention. It is wonder-

fully interactive, binding us together over great distances. It is v
reliable. And it doesn't have to be upgraded every six months.

The value of the telephone is not lost on Dorot, a nonprofit social
services organization for the elderly in New York City that runs,
among other activities, an educational program called University
Without Walls. Through telephone conference calls, it takes courses
and support-group sessions to older people and those with limited
mobility. "Some people say University Without Walls is their life,"
said Bonnie Jacobs, director of educational services at Dorot.
"They're either on the phone taking courses or talking to people
they met through the courses." The program allows Dorot (Hebrew
for "generations") to reach beyond its base in the New York metropolitan area. Some of its eight hundred students, who range in age
from forty to over one hundred, live in California, Florida, Iowa,
Maryland, Pennsylvania, and Vermont. One teacher conducts his
classes from his home in Switzerland. Information is available on
Dorot's Web site, www.dorotusa.org; prospective students can regis-
ter by calling Dorot in Manhattan at 1-212-769-2850 or toll-free at
1-877-819-9147.

Dorot offers a variety of noncredit courses covering literature,
history, science, and the arts, along with how-to classes and support-
group sessions for particular problems, like dealing with Medicare
or certain health or psychological difficulties. Many classes, fifty
minutes each, run once a week for a full fourteen-week semester.
Others last a few weeks, and some are single sessions. The registra-
tion fee is $10 a semester, plus a $15 charge for each course. There is
no charge for single-session classes, and Dorot waives fees for those
who have difficulty paying. It also pays all phone charges. Classes
may have just five students or as many as eighteen.

To participate, all a student has to do is be at the phone at the appointed time. When it rings, a staff member from the Dorot office
on the Upper West Side of New York is on the line to link him or her
to a conference call and to take roll. Then the teacher, or "facilita-
tor," takes over. After fifty minutes, the staff member breaks in and

announces that the class is over. For some courses, printed material is sent out in advance.

I participated in a class titled "The Glamour Gals and Guys of the '30s and '40s," which was taught by Bill Hubschmitt, a movie buff and semiretired accountant who lived in Sedona, Arizona. Clair, Sarah, Sally, Gilda, Pat, Linda, Eleanor, Evelyn, and Larry all responded to roll call before the class was turned over to Hubschmitt. The next fifty minutes were a trip back in time through a captivating, well-organized, and relatively in-depth discussion of the singers Alice Fay and Jane Powell, as well as an introduction to Judy Garland, a subject that would be carried over to the next week's class. The students were encouraged to chime in and express their opinions. Some did, but the presence of a stranger, and a journalist at that, might have inhibited the others.

Hubschmitt, who taught at Dorot for nearly a decade, said he thought his course was especially good for older students. "It's nostalgic for them and involves a lot of memory recall," he said. "Often they'll express an opinion about whether they liked or disliked a star. We agree to disagree. I think it helps to stimulate their minds."

After living and working in New York for sixty years, Hubschmitt moved to Arizona in 2001. He is a lifelong student of film and has more than three hundred silent films in his video collection. "I grew up in New York City in a large family," he said. "The only entertainment, the only escape from tenement life, was the movies, which I started going to when I was five or six."

Bonnie Jacobs, the director, says many people who take courses make friends with others in the class. "We encourage this," she said. "Sometimes they'll even create study groups outside of class."

Myrna Shapiro is a retired professor who divides her time between West Palm Beach, Florida, and Jericho, New York. She has been a University Without Walls student for seven years. She takes ten to twelve classes a semester. "I was a science major," she said, "and I especially enjoy the liberal arts courses." She added, "This program is a godsend for people with vision problems."

Zelda Hearst, seventy-five, a retired widow in Sunnyside, Queens, was a student and has taught several courses, including self-help ones like "Things I'm Afraid Of," "You're Getting on My Nerves," and "Mother-in-Law: Enemy or Ally." She made many telephone friends after she began teaching in 1994, including Myrna Shapiro, whom she has never met in person. "Sometimes the anonymity of phone friends is good and a special thing," she said. "It's like having an e-mail friend, only you can hear the person's voice, which I prefer. It's human contact. E-mail doesn't do much for me."

8

Social Security: Count on It

The most important thing we could do to protect
Social Security right now is leave it alone.
—MARK WEISBROT, COAUTHOR,
SOCIAL SECURITY: THE PHONY CRISIS

Many Americans think that the Social Security system is in deep trouble and needs major fixing or restructuring to "save" it from going broke. *Looming insolvency* is the term most often used in the media to describe the system's purported plight. Politicians issue dire warnings about the graying of America and the threat of generational warfare. Poll after poll reflects this concern among citizens; many young people say they expect they will never receive any Social Security benefits despite years of paying the tax. There is pressure to privatize the system, which would allow individuals to invest their Social Security taxes in the stock market.

Well, you can stop worrying.

None of these dire predictions is even remotely likely. And privatization might well do more harm than good. So-called reform of the Social Security system increasingly looks like a solution in search of a problem. What other issue can you think of, with a potential problem more than thirty years down the road, that has politicians so forcefully engaged?

Even under relatively gloomy economic forecasts, Social Security is rock-solid until 2041. With some minimal changes, it will be fine until 2081 or perhaps until the end of the century. That's assuming future economic growth is just half the annual average of about 3.5 percent over the past seventy-five years.

"The most important thing we could do to protect Social Security right now is leave it alone," said Mark Weisbrot, codirector of the Center for Economic and Policy Research in Washington, D.C., and coauthor with Dean Baker of *Social Security: The Phony Crisis* (University of Chicago Press, 2001).

Why all the fuss? Think hidden agendas, on all sides.

THE PUSH FOR PRIVATIZATION

Wall Street and its commission-driven brokers would love to get their hands on at least some of the $2 trillion in the Social Security trust fund, which is currently invested in United States government bonds. In its January 2002 issue, *Harper's Magazine* published an essay by Thomas Frank titled "The Trillion-Dollar Hustle: Hello Wall Street, Goodbye Social Security." It's an excellent short primer on Wall Street's push for privatization.

In addition, ultraconservative Republicans and others who are ideologically opposed to the whole concept of government-sponsored social insurance would like to fully privatize the system. Seeing that idea didn't fly politically, they have pushed—so far without success—for partial privatization, in which individuals would invest a portion of their Social Security tax in the stock market, all in the name of rescuing the system. The concept picked up some support across the political spectrum in the 1990s but lost a bit of steam when the stock market went south. The Bush administration tried to revive the idea, but that effort collapsed in 2005 in the face of immense public resistance. Nevertheless, it continues to simmer on political back burners and is sure to boil over again. Several variations remain under consideration, including the one modeled after individual retirement accounts that was championed by George W. Bush; it would give Americans broad discretion over how they invest their money.

The immediate problem with privatization is that Social Security is a pay-as-you-go system: today's retirees are supported by today's workers. The surplus in the trust fund is there to handle the bulge in the retiree population that will occur when the large numbers of baby boomers soon begin to collect their Social Security payments. Partial privatization would take up to a third of current revenues and put the money into private accounts. How would this money—more than $200 billion a year—be replaced so that current benefits could be paid? The government could increase taxes, take on more debt, or cut benefits—all unpleasant solutions to a problem that didn't need to be created in the first place.

Proponents of privatization don't like to be reminded that, as we have seen in recent years, stocks can go down as well as up. Weisbrot, an economist, points out that declines can be long term. Between 1968 and 1978, for example, the stock market lost 45 percent of its value. He and the Center for Economic and Policy Research (www.cepr.net) have calculated that if the most modest of the various privatization plans had been put into effect at the beginning of 1998, by November 1, 2002, the Social Security system would have lost $45 billion.

We'll look at some other difficulties with privatization later.

Bipartisan "Concern"

The exaggerations about Social Security's problems are coming not just from Republicans and other conservatives. Remember President Bill Clinton exhorting Congress to use the budget surplus to "save" Social Security instead of cutting taxes? The Democrats try to score political points by depicting themselves as the great saviors of Social Security. The Republicans aren't about to cry foul and say the system doesn't need saving. If they do, there goes their argument for privatization. "There's a kind of gentlemen's agreement here in Washington, I'm afraid, not to point out the basic fact that we don't really need to be talking about Social Security," Weisbrot said.

One of the biggest smoke screens in the debate is the idea that the Social Security "crisis" will cause generational conflicts as younger people are forced to support a growing older population. The argument conjures up images of old people with canes and walkers, barricaded in retirement villages, fighting off roving hoards of Generation Xers and Yers. Ari Fleischer, the former White House press secretary, said in a 2002 press briefing that as Social Security is currently structured, younger workers paying into the system would "get nothing back." He was later forced to retract that statement when some economists pointed out that it was in direct contradiction to the Social Security trustees' annual reports.

It's important to keep in mind that, as Knight A. Kiplinger writes in *World Boom Ahead: Why Business and Consumers Will Prosper* (Kiplinger Books, 1998), the graying of America will be very gradual. It may be true that by 2020 about 53 million people, or 16 percent of the population, will be over sixty-five, compared with the current 37.2 million, or 12.5 percent. But Kiplinger says that isn't the whole picture. Because of general population growth, including immigration, the number of young people will be growing, too, and the nation's median age in 2020 will be 38.1, not greatly less than the median age of Florida's current population: 39.6. The current national median age is 36.4.

Moreover, Generation Xers and Yers didn't spring full-grown from the mind of Tommy Hilfiger. They have parents and grandparents, too, and they want them to have secure retirements. Today's young people themselves will eventually retire. Polls by the 2030 Center, which studies economic issues affecting younger people, show broad support among young people for Social Security.

Here's a modest proposal. Since whatever problems Social Security may have are a very long way off, let's have a ten-year test of privatization—with congressional pensions. Let Congress pass a law linking representatives' and senators' pensions to the Standard

& Poor's 500 stock index. Maybe as Congress debates health care, it should force its members into HMOs. Both moves would, to borrow from Dr. Samuel Johnson, focus their minds wonderfully.

Good News from the Trustees

Every year the trustees of Social Security issue an annual report on the status of the system. The report covering 2006 was issued on Monday, April 23, 2007. It estimated that:

- The point at which tax revenues will fall below expenses, forcing the system to dip into its trust fund to pay benefits, will come in 2017, the same as the estimate in the previous year's report.
- The point at which the trust fund will be exhausted was put at 2041, one year later than 2040, projected in the previous year's report.

Oddly, the headline on the news release summarizing the report—"Long-Range Financing Challenges Continue"—seemed a tad pessimistic, given that a trustee report as recently as 1995 had put the date for the trust fund to be depleted at 2030. That's eleven years earlier than is expected in the report for 2006.

Sure, it is technically true that if nothing changes—if Social Security taxes are never increased no matter how much the economy grows—and if all economic and demographic projections are perfectly on target, then in 2041 the system will be able to pay out only 75 percent of scheduled benefits. That's a lot of ifs spread out over more than three decades.

The trustees' report actually peers seventy-five years into the future. To fill the gap created by the expiration of the trust fund in 2041 and keep the system going until 2081 would require an additional $4.7 trillion. That's $100 billion more than was estimated in the previous year's report.

That sounds like a lot of money, but it covers a seventy-five-year period. To put it in perspective, if we increased Social Security taxes today to fill that $4.7 trillion gap, the rise would have to be 1.95

percentage points, half to be paid by workers and half by employers. That would mean each would pay 7.18 percent; they now pay 6.2 percent. Of course, the longer we wait, the steeper the increase will have to be.

Raising the payroll tax is not the only alternative, however. Such an increase could be less if it were combined with an increase in the amount of a person's annual income that is subject to Social Security taxes. The ceiling for 2007, for example, was $97,500; if you earned more than that it was free of Social Security taxes. But raising the ceiling and making the tax less regressive would involve raising taxes on wealthier people—not a popular idea in Washington these days.

"If you were going to take the current system and fix it but not in a structural way—a little bit of this and a little bit of that—then raising the ceiling could certainly be in the mix," said John L. Palmer, one of two appointed public trustees for Social Security and Medicare. "It would increase benefits somewhat because they are calculated on a person's taxable base. But, on balance, it would improve the finances of the system. And it would make the tax more progressive."

All this, of course, is based on very long-term projections by a government that often has had trouble predicting budget surpluses and deficits a year or two in advance. "There is a tremendous amount of uncertainty in a seventy-five-year projection," conceded Palmer, who is an economist at the Maxwell School of Citizenship and Public Affairs at Syracuse University.

Mark Weisbrot of the Center for Economic and Policy Research says the idea of making predictions seventy-five years into the future is a "joke." "You may as well use a crystal ball," he said. "It's science fiction."

One Washington wag put it more bluntly: "Anybody who thinks they can make economic projections for seventy-five years from now ought not to be allowed on the street unassisted."

John Palmer says a lot of analysis goes into the Social Security projections, which fall mid-range between optimistic and pessimistic outlooks. However, there are plenty of economists who think the

Social Security projections are based on estimates that are too con-servative. This is important because if future economic growth is greater than projected by even a little, it has profoundly positive consequences for Social Security. The expected shortfalls can shrink or even vanish if growth is sufficient. Jeremy J. Siegel, a professor of finance at the Wharton School of the University of Pennsylvania and the author of *Stocks for the Long Run: The Definitive Guide to Financial Market Returns and Long-Term Investment Strategies* (McGraw-Hill, 2002), agrees that economic growth could go a long way toward solving Social Security's problems. Nevertheless, he fa-vors partial privatization, not because it will rescue the system but because he thinks it will encourage people to save.

It's not just the economy the trustees' projections take into ac-count. "A big driver for our long-term projections are birth rates and life expectancy," Palmer said. Lower birth rates and longer life ex-pectancy mean that there will be fewer young people paying into the system and those collecting benefits will collect them longer. Immi-gration is an important factor that can help offset declining birth rates.

The Government Borrowed Our Money

The Social Security system pays benefits out of current taxes with the surplus going into a trust fund, so there will be money available for the expected increase in future retirees as the baby boomers start collecting benefits. That trust fund, which is invested in gov-ernment bonds and is often misunderstood, has become a political football. Its expected depletion is cited by critics who want to "save" Social Security by privatizing it, or who are ideologically opposed to the concept of government-sponsored social insurance. That the fund is expected to start redeeming its bonds in 2017 to help pay benefits is often decried as a huge problem for Social Security be-cause the payout will come from the Treasury.

That's not Social Security's problem. It's a fiscal problem for the government, which has borrowed the money by issuing the bonds. Through 2006, the fund contained nearly $2 trillion in bonds, which earned interest of 5.3 percent that year—or $102 billion. If Congress doesn't want to repay the money, it shouldn't have borrowed it. To see the redemption of those bonds as Social Security's problem is akin to borrowing money from a bank and then, when the debt comes due, declaring it the bank's problem. Palmer agreed with that assessment, but noted that the exhaustion of the trust funds would be a Social Security problem. Also, the bonds aren't all going to be cashed in at once. They'll be gradually redeemed by Social Security as needed over two decades, assuming the projections are correct. If the past is any guide, the dates when the system is expected to face problems may continue to be extended.

Viewing those bonds as a Social Security problem also flirts with the assumption that the government might default on them, something that has never happened in the nation's history. A lot of people own government bonds; some rich people own a lot of them. "Ross Perot has invested in U.S. Treasury bonds, and nobody is talking about his not being paid," said Mark Weisbrot of the Center for Economic and Policy Research. "Why should millions of workers be treated any differently? These Social Security bonds carry the full faith and credit of the government. If they're not going to be paid, you may as well throw away that $20 bill in your pocket." He added: "The government took the money out of our checks, and put it in bonds. They happen to be government bonds. What if Social Security had invested this money in private corporate bonds? We wouldn't even be having this discussion. They would just be cashed in. Why should this be any different?"

Not a New Problem

Weisbrot also thinks the Social Security system is basically in good shape and that future problems will be minor and readily solved. "By 2042 people will be making more than 40 percent above what they make today, in real inflation-adjusted terms, according to the trustees' own projections," he said. "Is anyone really worried about paying an additional 1 percent of their income for a system that keeps our old people out of poverty? Maybe people who are ideologically opposed to the concept. But the Social Security tax has been raised by more than this in the past. The projected shortfalls are less than the shortfalls that were taken care of in the '50s, '60s, '70s, and '80s. The system is more sound than it's been throughout most of its sixty-seven-year history. These shortfall projections are based on the assumption that no taxes will ever be raised, no matter how rich the country gets over the next seventy-five years. That's three-quarters of a century. It's only under that assumption that you can say Social Security has any problem at all."

He said the entire projected shortfall for the next seventy-five years is less than 1 percent of our nation's gross domestic product—the total value of all goods and services—over the same period. "We have solved shortages before and there's every indication people would be willing to do it again," he said. "After all, it's not that it's such a small percentage of our income, but that our incomes are going to be so much higher that nobody will ever notice the difference. There's no possibility that anyone is going to suffer a reduced living standard if we have to fill that shortfall in the science fiction future."

He added: "People are being deceived. People who are leading the debate are being deceptive. I just wish the critics would be honest and tell people there is a small problem years down the road that can be easily fixed. That shortfall will be taken care of like those in the past. If it weren't for the powerful influence of Wall Street, which wants the commissions privatization would bring, and politically active ideologues, this wouldn't even be an issue."

The Perils of Privatization

The biggest, immediate, and most obvious problem with privatization is the deficit that would be created in the pay-as-you-go system as funds are diverted to private accounts.

The second obvious problem, as I mentioned, is that stocks fall as well as rise. Proponents of privatization often say that over the long term stocks are the best investment because they will deliver higher returns than bonds. Jeremy Siegel of the Wharton School expects market returns to be 5 to 7 percent, adjusted for inflation, over the next decade or so. Sometimes you see predictions of 11 or 12 percent, but they are almost always not adjusted for inflation. In truth, nobody can predict the future of the stock market. Who in the late 1980s saw the market surge of the 1990s?

Of course, investing for the long term is theoretically supposed to smooth out these bumps in the stock market. But your definition of long term depends on your age and when you plan to retire. If you dumped your savings into the stock market in the summer of 1929, you had better have been pretty young. The market's recovery from the October 1987 crash was much faster than from 1929's, but that wasn't much help if you had planned to retire that fall.

In their book *The Great 401(k) Hoax: Why Your Family's Financial Security Is at Risk, and What You Can Do About It* (Perseus Publishing, 2002), William Wolman and Anne Colamosca say that history suggests we face a stock market slump that could last for two decades. They expect annual returns over these years to average less than 2 percent, adjusted for inflation. That projection makes the Social Security trust fund's investment in government bonds, which paid 5.3 percent in 2006, look pretty sweet.

Winners and Losers

There are other, less obvious problems with privatization that are rooted in the kind of society we are, or aspire to be. Privatization, in which people would be free to invest some of their Social Security taxes in stocks as they wish, would inevitably create a system of winners and losers. Not all people are equally sophisticated at picking stocks or mutual funds. A Century Foundation project on Social Security has pointed out that without the system's guaranteed monthly benefits, about half the elderly in America would fall below the poverty line. Social Security was created to give everyone a base line, a solid floor of income protection. It has been one of the most successful social programs in our nation's history, keeping millions from falling into poverty. Retiree benefits are fully insured against market risks. Do we really want to create a society in which retirees' proximity to the poverty line is determined by their stock market savvy?

Besides retirement income, the Social Security system provides other benefits that could be at risk under privatization. These include insurance to support survivors of workers who die young, guaranteed income for the disabled, and protection from inflation through benefits that are indexed to rise with the cost of living. Also, the cost of administering the Social Security system is much less than private insurers and investment companies charge.

A privatized system would surely have to have some safeguards to protect novice investors from dangers like account-churning by commission-driven brokers, or from brokers who push dubious stock on which they receive an enhanced commission. ("What, you never heard of Southern Indiana Drywall? Well, a lot of people hadn't heard of Microsoft when it got started.") The Century Foundation has suggested that in order to protect workers from losing their retirement funds, most high-risk and novel investments should be ruled out. The catch-22 of such safeguards is that they might restrict people who are really good at investing. This entire proposal clearly needs more thought.

A More Productive Workforce

One of the most popular arguments used by critics of Social Security is that the number of workers available to support one retiree is declining to a dangerously low, and ultimately unsupportable, level. It was 3.3 in 2006 and is expected to drop to 2.2 by 2030, when the baby boomers will largely have retired. In 1945, there were 41.9 workers for each retiree; in 1955, 8.6; and in 1965, 4.0. From 1975 until 2002, the number remained fairly constant at 3.2 to 3.4. Projections by Social Security trustees call for the numbers to drop to 2.6 in 2020, 2.2 in 2030, 2.1 in 2040, and 1.8 in 2080.

However, as Weisbrot and Baker point out in *Social Security: The Phony Crisis*, these demographic and labor force statistics look scary because they are presented in isolation, out of context relative to other economic factors—and are thus more or less meaningless.

First, the authors say, we should look at the reduced burden workers will face as the birth rate declines. They write: "The increase in the future burden of caring for a larger elderly population will be offset to a large extent by the reduced costs of education, child care, and other expenses of caring for dependent children."

Second, they argue, these dire dependency ratios fail to take into account productivity increases. "To say that Social Security will go broke because of the declining number of workers per retiree is like saying that we should be very hungry right now because the percentage of the workforce in agriculture has declined from 5.1 to 1.1 over the last forty years," they write. "Just as we can now feed the nation and in fact export a large agricultural surplus with vastly fewer people employed in agriculture, it is also true that fewer workers can support a large number of retirees as the productivity of the entire economy grows."

The authors also say that the projected decline from 3.3 in 2006 to 2.2 in 2030 is less steep than the decline from 8.6 in 1955 to 3.3—and that drop did not precipitate an economic disaster.

Why Roll the Dice?

As the politicians and lobbyists in Washington strive to score political or ideological points in the Social Security debate, they should be aware that people like Edith Chvala are watching them. Like some economists, she questions the wisdom of staking Social Security funds on the stock market. Chvala, in her mid-eighties, lives in Tucson, Arizona, on $1,469 a month—$1,308 from Social Security and $161 from a pension.

As she has watched the struggle over Social Security, Chvala has come to at least one conclusion: she is not excited about proposals that would put a portion of the funds, now invested in Treasury securities, into the stock market—whether it's a plan for the government to invest the money or one allowing individuals to invest part of their Social Security tax payments themselves. "I'm not a gambler," she said. "It seems like they want to gamble with our retirement money."

A native of Germany, Chvala came to the United States in 1930, when she was seven. She grew up in New York City, living in Queens and then Sheepshead Bay, Brooklyn. She married in 1945 and followed her husband, a construction worker, around the Northeast. In 1970, they moved to Buffalo, New York, where she worked as a nurse's aid for twenty years. That job was the source of her small pension. The couple divorced in 1973; her former husband has since died.

At the urging of a son who lived there, she moved to the Southwest in 1990. She first moved to New Mexico, and then when her son relocated to Tucson she followed him there. But while health problems have forced Chvala to curtail her activities, she continues to live on her own. "I like my independence," she said. "My plan is just to drop dead—when the time comes." And in the meantime she would rather that politicians keep their hands off Social Security.

If You Were a Carpenter

Another move often suggested by Social Security's critics is to raise the retirement age to seventy or older for collecting full benefits. The argument is that people are living and working longer, and increasing the retirement age would save money for the system.

Whenever I hear policy strategists or ivory-tower academics proposing this, I can't help wishing they would get up from their ergonomically designed chairs and spend a day with some construction workers at a job site.

I talked to a carpenter and a laborer—both in their late thirties—working among the rising girders of an office building in New Jersey.

Their jobs are physically difficult, especially during the winter cold. And in their circle of workers, the idea of staying on the job until seventy is not exactly catching fire. "By the time you reach fifty-five or sixty in the heavy construction business, most contractors don't want you," the carpenter said. "You just can't do the hard work after years of getting banged around." The laborer pointed to a huge supermarket nearby. "The blocks they used to build that with weigh a hundred and five pounds each," he said. "I lifted ninety percent of them."

Both the carpenter and the laborer said there was pressure from contractors to keep working hard all day. "I've been on jobs where they get mad if you take too many drinks of water," the carpenter said. "It's go, go, go. If you don't feel good and slack off, that's no excuse." They work, often outside, in rain and snow. And they get paid only if they work. "There are no paid holidays, no vacation, no sick days," he said.

The two men also cited safety as an especially acute issue for older construction workers. The laborer should know. When he was twenty-nine, a scaffold on which he was working collapsed, sending him crashing twenty feet to a concrete floor. He suffered head injuries, his back was broken in three places, and his collarbone was fractured. "If I'd been sixty-six or sixty-seven, I'd have been done for," he said.

You don't have to spend much time talking with people like these two who build our buildings, pave our roads, or tote our trash to see clearly the contrast between them and people who work in comfortably heated and air-conditioned offices. Guess where those who make the retirement-policy decisions work.

The notion of retiring at sixty-five is already slipping away, at least as far as Social Security is concerned. Changes made by Congress in 1983 are ratcheting up the retirement age for people born after 1937 (see figure 11). Of course, no matter when you were born you can get permanently reduced Social Security payments at age sixty-two. Someone born in 1944 must wait an extra year, until they are sixty-six, to get full retirement benefits. If they work in an office, it

Figure 11

Social Security and Retirement Age

Changes to Social Security rules are gradually raising the age at which you may retire and receive full retirement benefits. You may still choose to retire sooner—starting at age 62—but, if you do, your benefits will be reduced according to a formula. Here are the minimum ages for full benefits, depending on the year in which you were born. (People born on January 1 are counted under the previous year.)

For people who were born in:	The **minimum age** to receive full benefits at retirement is:	The total reduction if you retire at age 62:	A $1,000 monthly benefit would be reduced to:
1937 or before	65	20.00%	$800
1938	65 years, 2 months	20.83	791
1939	65 years, 4 months	21.67	783
1940	65 years, 6 months	22.50	775
1941	65 years, 8 months	23.33	766
1942	65 years, 10 months	24.17	758
1943–1954	66	25.00	750
1955	66 years, 2 months	25.83	741
1956	66 years, 4 months	26.67	753
1957	66 years, 6 months	27.50	725
1958	66 years, 8 months	28.33	716
1959	66 years, 10 months	29.17	708
1960 or after	67	30.00	700

Source: Social Security Administration

won't be such a big deal to roll up to their keyboard for another year. But if they operate a jackhammer . . . "A big part of the push to increase the retirement age to seventy is simply that the policy crowd doesn't work at jobs in which they're spent by the time they're sixty-five," Weisbrot said. So the next time you hear someone calling for raising the retirement age to seventy, ask them what they do for a living.

UNDERSTANDING THE SYSTEM

Joe and Sue Sample, the hypothetical couple in chapter 2, plan to retire when they are sixty but cannot begin collecting even reduced Social Security benefits until they are sixty-two. They cannot collect

full benefits until they are sixty-six. (The full retirement age is from sixty-five to sixty-seven, depending on when you were born.)

However, if they stop working at sixty—or take part-time jobs or jobs that pay less than their former positions—they could face an even further, although perhaps slight, reduction in benefits, depending on their work history. That's because monthly benefits are based on an average of your highest thirty-five years of earnings, which are indexed for inflation to bring them up to current dollar amounts. If you don't have thirty-five years, zeros are used for each year you lack. Assuming that the Samples had thirty-three years of work and stopped working at sixty, when they applied for benefits at sixty-two, those last two years would count as zeros in calculating the average on which their benefits are based. Of course, if they had thirty-five years of work, there would be no zeros added. Even with thirty-five years of work, these final years can still be important if, like most people, your highest earning years are at the end of your career.

The longer you wait to retire, the greater your Social Security benefits will be. You just won't be able to collect them for as long. If you need the benefits as soon as possible, like the Samples, to make retirement work for you, then you have no choice. Remember, however, that if you take reduced benefits, they are reduced forever. Also remember that if you take benefits at sixty-two, these benefits can be reduced even more if you work and your earnings exceed a specified amount; at your full retirement age, the earnings limit ends. If you have enough money to retire and get by without Social Security, then you have a decision: take the benefits now or wait until you are older and they have grown considerably. Figure 11 shows when you can collect full retirement benefits and the penalty for retiring early.

In Joe Sample's case, for instance, at sixty-two he will get about $1,300 a month. If he waits until he is sixty-six, he'll get about $1,800 a month; at seventy, about $2,500. (For Sue, the figures are $900, $1,300, and $1,800.) However, these projected amounts are based on the assumption that Joe continues working until he collects them. If he retires and holds off taking the benefits, they'll grow somewhat less because of the thirty-five-year averaging. He will miss out on a few years of higher earnings in his average or face some zeros in his average if he falls short of thirty-five years.

When the stock market is making impressive gains, many financial advisers say that people should take the benefits as soon as possible, even if they don't need them, and invest the money. They figure you would be ahead of the game compared with leaving the money in the system and collecting an enhanced benefit when you are older. In a bear market, that advice is usually reversed. That's because if you were born in 1943 or later, the system will increase your retirement benefits 8 percent for every year you delay taking them until you are seventy. Eight percent is considered a modest return compared with a high-performing stock market; when the market slumps it's darned good.

The Social Security Web site (www.ssa.gov) has some online calculators to help you figure out which course is best.

The Basics of Social Security

The Social Security Web site provides a wealth of information about how the system works and its benefits to you. Its data are rock-solid and accepted (although interpreted differently) by all sides in the debate over the future of the system. Your annual statement showing your earnings record and estimated benefits is also of great value.

Here are some Social Security facts—all explained in greater detail on the Web site—that you should be clear on.

- The tax you pay for Social Security is 6.2 percent of your income, up to an annual limit that was $97,500 in 2007. Your employer pays another 6.2 percent, for a total of 12.4 percent. If you are self-employed, you must pay the entire 12.4 percent.
- That annual salary limit for Social Security taxes rises each year based on increases in the national average wage.

- If you take early retirement benefits at sixty-two, they will be reduced by a percentage that depends on the age at which you are eligible for full benefits. The closer you are to full-benefit age, the less they are reduced. If your full retirement age is sixty-five, and you retire at sixty-two, your monthly benefits will be reduced by about 20 percent; at sixty-three, about 13.3 percent; and at sixty-four, about 6.7 percent. If your full retirement age is sixty-seven, and you retire at sixty-two, your benefits will be lowered by 30 percent; at sixty-three, 25 percent; at sixty-four, 20 percent; at sixty-five, 13.3 percent; and at sixty-six, 6.7 percent.

- If you retire early and decide to take a part-time job or freelance on your own, be wary of some short-term limits on earnings that will reduce your Social Security benefits. If you are less than your full retirement age, $1 in benefits will be deducted for each $2 you earn above an annual limit that was $12,960 in 2007. In the year you reach your full retirement age, $1 in benefits will be deducted for each $3 you earn above a more generous limit that was $34,400 in 2007. When you hit full retirement age, all limits disappear; you can earn as much as you want with no benefit reductions. Obviously, if you plan to work in retirement and will have enough money to live on, you might be better off delaying collecting Social Security until your full retirement age.

- You can collect Social Security benefits if you live abroad. However, you generally cannot have access to Medicare benefits overseas.

Your Social Security Statement

Pay particular attention to the annual statement you receive from the Social Security Administration. You can also request a statement anytime from the Social Security Web site.

The annual statement shows your earnings record. It can be a trip down memory lane. My statement shows that in 1959, when I was a high school freshman, I earned $358. I think that was from working for a public library in Indiana.

The statement also shows what your monthly benefits will be at age sixty-two and at your full retirement age, based on your earnings history and the assumption that you continue working until you retire. It also shows how much you would get right now if you were disabled, as well as what your family's benefits would be if you died. People I talked to who haven't paid much attention to their annual statement are often pleasantly surprised by the amounts they'll receive. Some even start thinking about early retirement.

9

Putting It All Together

I either answer their questions or tell them where they can get answers.
— JIM MILLER, COLUMNIST, "THE SAVVY SENIOR"

Richard Mayer, the Mineola, New York, financial consultant, stresses the importance of looking closely at your financial situation before you make retirement decisions. To that end, he has provided blueprints for calculating expenses and net worth. He separates expenses into five broad categories: automobile, home, insurance, personal, and taxes. He then calculates expense items under each category three ways: preretirement; postretirement in your current location; and postretirement in a new, and presumably less expensive, location. Many preretirement expenses will be less or disappear altogether when you retire, especially if you move to the cheaper location. This is especially true for mortgage payments, multiple car expenses, and taxes. Figure 12 allows you to work through the three scenarios with your own numbers. To calculate expenses in a new location, use data provided by BestPlaces.net and RetirementLiving.com.

Figure 13 allows you to calculate your net worth. At the end of the chart, debts must be subtracted from total assets to arrive at your bottom line.

Figure 12

Worksheet: Monthly Expenses

	Before retiring	After retiring (same location)	After retiring (new location)
Automobile expenses			
Loan or lease payment			
Fuel			
Repairs			
License and registration			
Other			
Expenses for your home			
Mortgage or rent payment			
Electric service			
Gas service			
Fuel oil			
Cable/satellite TV service			
Telephone service—local			
Long distance calling			
Mobile phone			
Water			
Lawn and landscaping			
Association dues			
Other			
Taxes			
Federal income tax			
State income tax			
County income tax			
City income tax			
Real estate tax			
Sewer tax			
Water tax			
School tax			
Other			
Subtotal for this page			

(continued)

Worksheet: Monthly Expenses

	Before retiring	After retiring (same location)	After retiring (new location)
Personal expenses			
Allowance/spending money			
Boat			
Charitable giving			
Clothing and shoes			
Continuing education			
Computer and related			
Cosmetics			
Credit card payments			
Dry cleaning			
Hair care			
Hobbies			
Jewelry			
Club memberships			
Professional dues			
Travel			
Second home			
Subscriptions			
Pets and veterinary			
Food:			
At home			
Restaurants			
Gifts:			
Birthdays			
Holidays			
Other gifts			
Other expenses			
Subtotal for this page			

(continued)

Worksheet: Monthly Expenses

	Before retiring	After retiring (same location)	After retiring (new location)
Insurance			
Automobile			
Homeowners			
Life insurance			
Long-term care			
Mortgage			
Umbrella			
Health:			
Doctor and surgical			
Hospital			
Prescriptions			
Unreimbursed:			
Copayments			
Deductibles			
Dental			
Eyes and glasses			
Hearing			
Medicines			
Other			
Subtotal for this page			
Subtotal from first page			
Subtotal from second page			
Grand total			

Source: Richard E. Mayer

Figure 13

Worksheet: Net Worth

	Bank	Brokerage	Credit union	Life insurance	Total
Cash and liquid assets					
Checking					
Savings					
Money market					
C.D.s					
Treasuries					
Cash value					
Bonds					
Stocks					
Mutual funds					
Annuities					
I.R.A.s					
401(k)					
403(b)					
457					
Profit sharing					
Money purchase					
Pension					
Other accounts					
Subtotal: Cash and liquid assets					

	Estimated value		Estimated value
Personal assets			
Artwork		Jewelry	
Antiques		Collectibles	
Furniture and furnishings		Others	
Precious metals			
Subtotal: Personal assets			

	Gross value	Less: Money owed to other parties	Net value
Businesses and partnerships			
C Corporations			
Partnerships			
Sole proprietor			
Subtotal: Businesses and partnerships			

(continued)

Worksheet: Net Worth

	Gross value	Less: amount of loan outstanding	Net value
Major assets with outstanding debts			
Primary residence			
Second residence			
Unimproved land			
Rental property			
Boat			
R.V.			
Automobiles			
Subtotal: Major assets with outstanding loans			

	Amount owed		Amount owed
Other debts			
Lines of credit		Federal taxes	
Life insurance loans		State taxes	
Credit card balances		Local taxes	
Student loans		Other	
Personal loans			
Other loans			
		Subtotal: Other debts	

Adding it all up

From first page:	Cash and liquid assets	
	Personal assets	
	Businesses and partnerships	
From this page:	Major assets with outstanding debts +	
	Assets subtotal	
From this page:	Less: Other debts −	
	Your net worth is:	

Source: Richard E. Mayer

Finally, of course, you need to calculate your retirement income, much as the Samples did in chapter 2. The value of first charting your net worth is that you may be able to see ways to use some of it to produce income. For instance, if you sell an expensive house and move to a cheaper property, you may have some money left over. You might want to use it to buy an annuity or some other kind of income-producing investment. Although pension income continues to shrink as companies cut back and force employees to rely more on 401(k) plans, for most people the three sources of income in retirement will be a pension, Social Security, and income from investments, including 401(k) plans.

Figures 14 and 15 will help you select a health insurance plan and cut prescription drug costs. Since health insurance will likely be one of the few expenses that increase after retirement, you will want to pay special attention to this part of your budget.

Now you need to put it all together. You know your monthly expenses whether you retire and stay put or move to a new place. You know your net worth. And you know your income. Does it work?

"WHY DIDN'T I THINK OF THAT?"

I decided to end this book with an account of Jim Miller—in his mid-forties—because he is a perfect illustration of the value of a clever idea; the importance of following your bliss, as Joseph Campbell advises; and the value of thinking small. Miller was the subject of one of my "Seniority" columns in the *New York Times* under the heading "The Senior Discount, as Applied by a Writer." One reader lamented in an e-mail, "Why didn't I think of that?"

Living in Norman, Oklahoma, Miller—in his midforties—writes a weekly, self-syndicated column called "The Savvy Senior" that runs in more than four hundred mostly small daily and weekly newspapers around the country. Here's the part about thinking small: he

Figure 14

Worksheet: Choosing the Health Plan for You

Your family medical status (including pre-existing conditions):

Expected medical expense needs:

☐ Relatively healthy

☐ Hospitalization, surgery, or ongoing medical / lab treatments

☐ Frequent doctor's office visits

☐ Brand-name drug treatments

☐ Chronic medical condition

☐ Other:

Your primary goals:

☐ Low premium

☐ Low deductible

☐ Copayments rather than coinsurance

☐ Prescription drug coverage with low copay / coinsurance

☐ Low out-of-pocket annual maximum / high lifetime benefit cap

☐ Other:

Location 1: **Your Home State**	HMO A	HMO B	PPO A	PPO B	HSA A	HSA B
Monthly premium x 12 =	$	$	$	$	$	$
Annual premium	$	$	$	$	$	$
Annual deductible +	$	$	$	$	$	$
Annual cost baseline (premium + deductible)	$	$	$	$	$	$
Scope of benefits:						
Co-pay (if applicable)	$	$	$	$	$	$
Coinsurance (if appl.)	$	$	$	$	$	$
Prescription drug coverage:						
Your medicines covered?	Yes No	Yes No	Yes No	Yes No	Yes No	Yes No
Co-pay (if applicable)	$	$	$	$	$	$
Coinsurance (if appl.)	$	$	$	$	$	$
Out-of-pocket maximum, after deductible	$	$	$	$	$	$
Lifetime benefit cap	$	$	$	$	$	$

Location 2:

Neighboring State	HMO A	HMO B	PPO A	PPO B	HSA A	HSA B
Monthly premium	$	$	$	$	$	$
x 12 =						
Annual premium	$	$	$	$	$	$
Annual deductible +	$	$	$	$	$ *	$ *
Annual cost baseline (premium + deductible)	$	$	$	$	$	$
Scope of benefits:						
Co-pay (if applicable)	$	$	$	$	$	$
Covers:						
Coinsurance (if appl.)	$	$	$	$	$	$
Covers:						
Prescription drug coverage:						
Your medicines covered?	Yes No	Yes No	Yes No	Yes No	Yes No	Yes No
Co-pay (if applicable)	$	$	$	$	$	$
Coinsurance (if appl.)	$	$	$	$	$	$
Out-of-pocket maximum, after deductible	$	$	$	$	$	$
Lifetime benefit cap	$	$	$	$	$	$

Worksheet: Calculating the Value of an HSA

Federal tax rate		State tax rate (if applicable)		Total estimated tax rate
___ %	+	___ %	=	___ %

HSA annual funding amount

*Match to an amount up to the policy's deductible (maximum of $2,700 per year for an individual, or $5,450 per year for a family)   x $ _____

HSA annual savings   = $ _____

Figure 15

Worksheet: Cutting Prescription Drug Costs

Prescription 1:	Pharmacy A:		Pharmacy B:		Pharmacy C:	
	30-day supply cost	Shipping if any	30-day supply cost	Shipping if any	30-day supply cost	Shipping if any
Price at prescribed dosage	$	$	$	$	$	$
Can the pill be split?	Yes	No				
Price at twice the prescribed dosage ÷ 2	– $	$	$	$	$	$
Savings	$	$	$	$	$	$

Prescription 2:	Pharmacy A:		Pharmacy B:		Pharmacy C:	
	30-day supply cost	Shipping if any	30-day supply cost	Shipping if any	30-day supply cost	Shipping if any
Price at prescribed dosage	$	$	$	$	$	$
Can the pill be split?	Yes	No				
Price at twice the prescribed dosage ÷ 2	– $	$	$	$	$	$
Savings	$	$	$	$	$	$

Prescription 3:	Pharmacy A:		Pharmacy B:		Pharmacy C:	
	30-day supply cost	Shipping if any	30-day supply cost	Shipping if any	30-day supply cost	Shipping if any
Price at prescribed dosage	$	$	$	$	$	$
Can the pill be split?	Yes	No				
Price at twice the prescribed dosage ÷ 2	– $	$	$	$	$	$
Savings	$	$	$	$	$	$

Prescription 4:	Pharmacy A:		Pharmacy B:		Pharmacy C:	
	30-day supply cost	Shipping if any	30-day supply cost	Shipping if any	30-day supply cost	Shipping if any
Price at prescribed dosage	$	$	$	$	$	$
Can the pill be split?	Yes	No				
Price at twice the prescribed dosage + 2	– $	$	$	$	$	$
Savings	$	$	$	$	$	$

Prescription Log

	Prescription 1	Prescription 2
Name		
Dosage		
Frequency		
Rx date		
Number of refills		
End of Rx date		
Filled-by pharmacy		
Pharmacy phone		
Checked Rx interactions		

	Prescription 3	Prescription 4
Name		
Dosage		
Frequency		
Rx date		
Number of refills		
End of Rx date		
Filled by pharmacy		
Pharmacy phone		
Checked Rx interactions		

charges $3 to $10 a week for his column, depending on a paper's circulation. "For a lot of small newspapers, three dollars a week is quite a bit of money," said Miller, who started selling the column in 2002. "Some of them are barely scraping by. I don't charge much because I want to reach a lot of people."

The column, at five hundred words, usually consists of a reader's question on an issue affecting older Americans and Miller's answer. Chatty and very informative, each column invites readers to submit questions by e-mail or regular mail. "Great idea!" he tells a reader who says her husband has been "spending too darn much time around the house" and is looking for a way for both of them to do volunteer work. Readers are directed to his free Web site (www.savvysenior.org), where they can also submit questions, read recent columns, and find links to other helpful sites for older people. He receives up to thirty questions a week, he said, many dealing with Social Security or Medicare. He responds to each. "I either answer their questions or tell them where they can get answers," he said.

The four hundred papers that run his column have a combined circulation of 7 million with a potential 20 million readers. The biggest are the *Las Vegas Review-Journal* and the *Richmond Times-Dispatch* in Virginia, both of which have Sunday circulations of more than 200,000; the smallest are some rural weekly papers with circulations of fewer than 1,500, like the *Forum* in Floodwood, Minnesota, and the *Stafford Courier* in Stafford, Kansas. Despite the column's tiny price, Miller said he made about $50,000 a year after expenses and before taxes.

He started writing a column about older people three years ago after his mother and father died within three weeks of each other. "That really shook me up," he said. "So I got involved with older people at a retirement community here in Norman. I thought it would help me get through the grieving process." The column was first published free in the *Norman Transcript*, which has a daily circulation of about 16,500. Soon, other papers in the area expressed an interest.

Miller decided to try selling the column around the country. He sent letters and sample columns to sixty-two hundred of the roughly twelve thousand daily and weekly papers in the United States. One of those who responded was Raymond Linex II, the editor of the *Corsicana Daily Sun* in Corsicana, Texas. His paper runs the column every Wednesday, and he says it is popular with his town's large number of older people. But Linex said the deciding factor was the price. "We wouldn't have been able to run the column if it hadn't been so affordable for us," he added. "We're in a very tight ad market." Linex said his paper planned to stick with "The Savvy Senior." "We have a need for that kind of column because there's nobody on our staff who can write it," he said. "And the price is just perfect for us."

Patricia St. Louis, the managing editor of the *Fountain Valley News,* a weekly newspaper in Fountain, Colorado, also bought the column. She praises it for the help it provides readers on issues like Medicare. She described it as a "good, important column that is full of information and resources. But I jumped on it because of the price," she added. "It's worth four or five times that."

Miller, who has become a regular on NBC's *Today* show, said he wanted to continue selling his column to newspapers. "I want to provide a service for seniors," he said. "I started the column with the idea of helping older people. I like older people and always have. Doing this column is gratifying. People are always grateful, because a lot of them just don't know where to turn. A lot of stuff we take for granted can be very complicated to older people. There's so much information for them to deal with. Many times they hear about something on television and have questions about it."

Miller is a native of Independence, Kansas, and has an undergraduate degree in education from Kansas State University and a graduate degree in education from Wichita State University. He worked for eight years in operations and events for the University of Oklahoma's athletic department in Norman before turning to his column. He is the stadium announcer for the university's football and basketball games—which he describes as a "part-time hobby job"—and was the announcer for gymnastics at the 1996 Summer Olympic Games in Atlanta.

"I started 'The Savvy Senior' for fun," he said. "But a lot of people have responded to it. It's amazing how many seniors are isolated and don't know where to turn for help."

ON THE WEB

www.aarp.org/revmort is the AARP Web site for just about everything you might want to know about reverse mortgages.

www.agu.net has some of the best and most current information on high-risk health insurance pools in the states that offer them. The site is run by Affinity Group Underwriters.

www.bestplaces.net is one of the best Internet sites for retirement planning. It allows you to compare not only cost-of-living data but information on housing, crime, education, economics, health, and climate.

It also has a calculator that allows you to figure how much income you would need to maintain your current lifestyle in another city or region. Another section of the site allows you to list your preferences for the above categories; it will then produce a list of cities that match your description of what you are looking for in a place to live.

www.bloggingawaydebt.com can be a helpful site if you're trying to cut expenses to pay down debt.

www.bloomberg.com has some good "what if" calculators that allow you to see, among other things, the advantages of prepaying a mortgage. The site is operated by Bloomberg News.

www.cahi.org is the site of the Council for Affordable Health Insurance, an advocacy group for insurers, which lists state mandates for insurance coverage.

www.cepr.net is the Web site of the Center for Economic Policy Research in Washington. It has a lot of good data relevant to the Social Security debate.

www.the-dma.org/consumers is the site of the Direct Marketing Association. It allows you to remove your name from its members' mailing lists.

www.dorotusa.org is the site for Dorot, the New York nonprofit social services organization that runs University Without Walls, described in chapter 7.

www.ehealthinsurance.com is excellent for health insurance information and for purchasing individual policies.

www.familyfight.com is a site run by Canadian lawyer Les Kotzer that offers advice on avoiding family fights over estates and incapacitated family members.

www.grandmabetty.com is a quirky but interesting site operated by Betty Fox, a grandmother in Queens. It offers a little bit of everything, including some good links to other sites as well as information on how to stretch your dollars and get free products.

www.healthinsuranceinfo.net is run by the Georgetown University Health Policy institute and provides current information on insurance rules in various states.

www.kff.org is run by the Kaiser Family Foundation and provides comprehensive health care data on the states. The site was primarily designed for health policy researchers and policy makers, according to Larry Levitt, vice president of the foundation. "But now we find that everyday consumers are using it as well," he said.

www.mathsisfun.com is for people who can't remember the finer points of high school or college math or are trying to come to grips with math terms that often appear in financial data and articles.

www.mightybargainhunter.com is a good site for those looking to cut expenses and save money.

www.movinon.net is popular with retirees interested in traveling in a recreational vehicle.

www.nahu.org is run by the National Association of Health Underwriters and can help you find an independent insurance broker in your area.

www.naic.org is the site of the National Association of Insurance Commissioners, a group that assists states in dealing with insurance regulations and has links to the various state insurance departments.

www.ofheo.gov is the Web site of the Office of Federal Housing Enterprise Oversight, a government agency that tracks changes in home values.

www.phrma.org is operated by the Pharmaceutical Research and Manufacturers of America. It is an excellent source of information on free prescription medicines from drug companies.

www.practicalmoneyskills.com is a really good site for basic help on personal finances.

www.propertyshark.com helps you research vital data, like ownership, sale prices, and taxes, on property in the United States.

www.realtor.com is a great site for looking at homes for sale around the country. It's operated by the National Association of Realtors.

www.retirementliving.com is best at comparing the taxes imposed by each state. It also has links to news sources and publications about seniors and retirement. There is a directory of state agencies that deal with issues of aging, and visitors to the site can sign up for a free e-mail newsletter.

The site also has sections on retirement communities and senior housing, as well as products and services. One warning: those offering housing, services, and products have not been evaluated by the site; they are simply there because they have paid a fee.

www.savvysenior.org is the Web site of Jim Miller, whose column called "The Savvy Senior" runs in more than four hundred small daily and weekly newspapers around the country. You can read recent columns and send Miller questions through the site.

www.smartmoney.com, operated by *Smart Money* magazine, is helpful with real estate and other financial issues.

www.ssa.gov is the Web site operated by the Social Security Administration. It provides an enormous amount of information on rules and benefits. Its data are rock-solid and accepted by all sides in the political debate over Social Security's future. You can use the site to request an estimate of your benefits, or you can calculate your own. This latter feature is important to early retirees, because it allows them to find out exactly how much their benefits will be reduced if they retire prior to their full retirement age.

www.taxfoundation.org is a good source of information on property taxes.

www.2young2retire.com is a fascinating site for retirees and those with aspirations to retire. It is operated by Howard and Marika Stone. Among other things, the site contains stories about people who, instead of accepting traditional retirement, have made transitions to new and what they consider more interesting careers and lifestyles. The Goldens, the couple in chapter 4 who spent time on the road in a motor home before settling down, were first featured here.

The Web site is the Stones' equivalent of the Goldens' Winnebago. Howard, sixty-eight, left a marketing career at a publisher, while Marika, sixty-two, is a former freelance business writer who now teaches yoga. Howard said: "I was tired of the pace of business and all that business travel, but the idea of retirement didn't really appeal to me. At the same time, I wanted to be involved in something that would make a difference. I think the Web site has turned out to be a help to people, because it tells stories that relate to their changing concerns and aspirations."

The Stones have also published a book, *Too Young to Retire: 101 Ways to Start the Rest of Your Life* (Plume, 2004).

www.zillow.com gives you an estimated value on your home or one you're thinking of buying, along with a satellite-eye view of the property. The site is a work in progress, so not all addresses are listed.

OFF THE SHELF

Age Works: What Corporate America Must Do to Survive the Graying of the Work Force (Free Press, 2002), by Beverly Goldberg, makes the case for retaining and hiring older workers.

Cities Ranked & Rated: More Than 400 Metropolitan Areas Evaluated in the U.S. and Canada (2nd edition, Wiley Publishing, 2007), by Bert Sperling and Peter Sander, is not specifically aimed at retirees but provides rankings and detailed information that can be very useful for retirement planning. Sperling runs the BestPlaces.net Web site.

Critical Condition: How Health Care in America Became Big Business—and Bad Medicine (Broadway, 2005), by Donald L. Barlett and James B. Steel, is a stunning and frightening exposé of the American health care system's shortcomings by two of the country's top investigative reporters.

The $800 Million Pill: The Truth Behind the Cost of New Drugs (University of California Press, 2005), by Merrill Goozner, answers the question: Why do prescription drugs cost so much? Hint: It's not because drug companies spend so much money on research.

The Family Fight: Planning to Avoid It (Continental Atlantic Publications, 2002), by Les Kotzer and Barry Fish, guides you through estate planning and arrangements for dealing with a family member who is incapacitated.

Generations: The History of America's Future, 1584 to 2069 (Harper Perennial, 1992), by William Strauss and Neil Howe, is *the* book to read for understanding generational issues and how they play out in our history and public policy.

The Great 401(k) Hoax: Why Your Family's Financial Security Is at Risk, and What You Can Do About It (Basic Books, 2003), by William Wolman and Anne Colamosca, is a scathing attack on the idea, much ballyhooed by Wall Street, that 401(k) plans linking workers' retirement well-being to the stock market are an easy way to amass wealth.

The authors remind us that these so-called defined-contribution plans were created to replace traditional defined-benefit pension plans not to empower or enrich workers but to relieve corporations of the expense and responsibility of funding and maintaining traditional pensions that are protected and guaranteed under federal law.

Companies may or may not match employee 401(k) contributions, but to the extent they do so with company stock it's even cheaper—never mind the financial risk to employees (remember Enron). When employees retire, they take their 401(k) money and that's that. A company has no pesky long-term commitments to retirees. All this is great for the corporate bottom line.

In the end, the authors say, many lower-paid workers are simply not able to save enough in 401(k) plans to give them sufficient money in retirement, especially if the stock market is in a long slump. Privatizing Social Security would make things even worse, they assert, turning a sure thing into a stock market bet.

What do they think we should do? For starters, they call for workers to have unrestricted investment choices for their 401(k) plans. They also think company matches should be in cold cash, not stock. They urge workers to shift investment to fixed-income securities.

Longevity Revolution: As Boomers Become Elders (Berkeley Hills Books, 2001), by Theodore Roszak, is an excellent antidote to the gloom-and-doom many writers and commentators associate with the graying of America. Roszak sees the aging population as a reason to celebrate, not worry; he sees opportunity where some others see disaster.

The Pill Book (12th edition, Bantam, 2006), by Harold M. Silverman, is a handy, often-updated reference for nonprofessionals that includes descriptions of drug interactions to help you juggle prescriptions filled by multiple pharmacies. Keep in mind that you should also consult your doctor and can ask for help from your pharmacist, whether or not you go to one drugstore for all of your prescriptions.

Retire in Style: 60 Outstanding Places Across the USA and Canada
(Next Decade, 2005), by Warren R. Bland, provides economic and
lifestyle information on the author's choices of good retirement
spots, based on a number of categories, including quality of life,
cost of living, health care, transportation, and cultural activities.

Retirement on a Shoestring (5th edition, Globe Pequot Press, 2004),
by John Howells, is filled with strategies for making your retirement money go as far as possible. It is written for people who
don't have plump pensions or 401(k) plans and may have to live
pretty much off Social Security. It gives down-to-earth advice on
cutting expenses and looks beyond the "best places" often cited in
books and magazine articles to even cheaper, but acceptable,
towns and areas. It covers topics from medical insurance and expenses to the pros and cons of retiring to less expensive areas
overseas.

Social Security: The Phony Crisis (University of Chicago Press,
2001), by Dean Baker and Mark Weisbrot, is a valuable guide for
anyone who is nervous or confused over the political discourse
about the future of Social Security. The authors, both liberal
economists, argue convincingly that because of overly conservative economic projections, Social Security is not in danger and
doesn't need to be saved by putting some of its funds into individual stock market accounts, as President George W. Bush and many
conservatives advocate. They see the drive to privatize Social Security as coming from ideologues who have never liked the system
and would like to diminish or destroy it, as well as from Wall Street
brokerage firms eager for the huge commissions such stock accounts would generate.

*Take Control with Your 401(k): An Employee's Guide to Maximizing
Your Investments* (Dearborn Trade Publishing, 2002), by David L.
Wray, does not take issue with the 401(k) concept. After all, the
author is president of the Profit Sharing/401(k) Council of America. But it does offer practical advice for managing your 401(k) retirement account and exercising your options. From opening an

account to cashing out, the details, rules, and terms are clearly explained.

You: The Smart Patient: An Insider's Guide for Getting the Best Treatment (Free Press, 2006), by Michael F. Roizen and Mehmet C. Oz. This second book by the best-selling authors of *You: The Owner's Manual* offers tips for being better informed about your medical condition and includes sample forms for recording personal and family medical histories.

Index

about the author

FRED BROCK, a former business editor and current contributor to *The New York Times*, is the author of *Health Care on Less Than You Think* and *Live Well on Less Than You Think* and holds the R. M. Seaton Professional Journalism chair at Kansas State University. He has also been an editor and reporter covering politics, business, and finance for *The Wall Street Journal*, the *Houston Chronicle*, and the *Louisville Courier-Journal*. He lives in Manhattan, Kansas.

You Can Have a Better Lifestyle Without a Bigger Paycheck
Learn How in These No-nonsense Guides from Fred Brock
Available in paperback from Times Books

Retire on Less Than You Think, Second Edition

In this indispensable guide, *New York Times* columnist Fred Brock cuts through the mutual-fund industry hype and Social Security scares to deliver frank and pragmatic advice on retirement planning. The book offers the latest thinking on all the essentials for a smart and secure retirement from finding untapped asset streams to building a reasonable budget based on your new lifestyle. It also includes a substantial list of national, regional, and online resources.

Live Well on Less Than You Think

Fred Brock challenges conventional financial wisdom again in this smart, down-to-earth primer on financial survival—and prosperity—in today's uncertain economy. Here Brock contests the hype that is driving money decisions during the working years—credit card debt, children's education costs, stagnant wages—and shows readers how to analyze their true costs of living so that they can live debt- and worry-free while enjoying themselves and securing their future.

Health Care on Less Than You Think

Drawing on his tested, popular strategies, Fred Brock tackles the most alarming financial issue facing Americans: the health care crisis. In this one-stop guide to maximizing your coverage while minimizing your costs—with potential savings of thousands of dollars each year—he shows how to shop for coverage based on location, manage Medicare to protect your retirement, assess the value of health savings accounts, track down savings on prescription drugs, and more.

Learn more about these books by visiting www.henryholt.com.